WRITERS FROM SOUTH AFRICA

FOURTEEN WRITERS ON CULTURE, POLITICS AND LITERARY THEORY AND ACTIVITY IN SOUTH AFRICA TODAY

A symposium held at Northwestern University
in conjunction with the publication of
*TriQuarterly #69, From South Africa: New Writing,
Photographs and Art*

David Bunn
Neville Choonoo
Ingrid de Kok
Keorapetse Kgositsile
Daniel P. Kunene
Mazisi Kunene
Anne McClintock

Njabulo S. Ndebele
Rob Nixon
Alfred Temba Qabula
Sheila Roberts
Ari Sitas
Jane Taylor
Hein Willemse

TriQuarterly Books

TriQuarterly Series on Criticism and Culture, No. 2

Reginald Gibbons, Editor, *TriQuarterly*
Arnold R. Weber, President, Northwestern University

Recordings of this conference were provided to Tri-Quarterly Books by the Office of University Relations, Northwestern University, Ken Wildes, Director. The recordings were transcribed by Janet Geovanis, edited by Reginald Gibbons and prepared for publication by Bob Perlongo. Type was set by Wendy Ward of Northwestern University's Academic Computing and Networking Services, George Sadowsky, Director.

Cover painting: "Lobola" by Alfred Thoba, oil on board, 84 x 63.5 cm (approximately 33" x 25"), 1987. Reproduced by permission of the Goodman Gallery, Johannesburg, South Africa. Thanks to Sue Williamson for locating this work.

Cover design by Gini Kindziolka.

Published by TriQuarterly Books
Northwestern University
2020 Ridge Avenue, Evanston, Illinois 60208

ISBN # 0-916384-03-9

CONTENTS

Linocut by Hamilton Budaza.

FOREWORD

What follows is the edited transcript of a conference that brought fourteen South African writers and critics to Northwestern University on October 30, 1987 to engage in a day of discussion and debate in two panel sessions, followed by a major address given by Njabulo S. Ndebele. One of the most notable aspects of the conference was that the participants tended to regard it not so much as the occasion to present a final word on matters, or even to develop a provisional position, but more as an opportunity to identify and sketch out for each other, as well as for the audience, the necessary subjects for debate. That is, this event was very much a small part in a larger and ongoing discussion, proceeding inside South Africa today, of culture and literature and politics. But a forum like this one could not have taken place in South Africa under apartheid. In fact, the opportunity it provided was especially rare in bridging the distances of exile for the participants, seven of whom came from South Africa and the other seven from residences in the United States and other countries. Crossing differences of race, gender, generation and experience, the fourteen were engaged in constructing, perhaps at times informally but in a lively and impressively thoughtful and learned way, an outline for the consideration of literary culture in South Africa, and even for future projects of literary creation there.

This lightly edited transcription of their remarks is offered to the reading public in the same spirit: not as a definitive assessment of literary culture in South Africa, but as a part of that literary culture—a collaborative working-out of many ideas and problems, punctuated by quotation or the recitation of poems here and there. Unfortunately, the most magnificent experience of the day—hearing the chanted poems of Alfred Temba Qabula—cannot be represented on paper.

It would be impossible to look at South African literature without considering seriously the political system and the effect it has on writers, as on all people who must exist under its restrictions—on the subjects they think about, the ways they conduct their lives and work, and even the forms in which they extend their insights to each other. One thing that the conference made clear is how resourceful and broad literary culture has become in response to the needs of people living under apartheid. Alfred Qabula, for example, is a factory worker and union organizer who has developed new artistic possibilities through participating in the rich and allusive tradition of the *imbongi*, or praise-singer. He conceives his poems not for publication but for performance, at union meetings, rallies and other public gatherings, where the audience might range from a small room of people to a stadium filled to capacity. Most, if not all, of the South African writers attending the conference obviously regarded Qabula's poetry as part of a significant and increasing trend in grass-roots activity, in which cultural as well as political efforts are directed at achieving democratic ideals.

Since the conference met in October 1987, however, several new restrictions have been enacted by the government in South Africa. In February 1988, it banned the activities of seventeen leading antiapartheid organizations, including the United Democratic Front (UDF), and prohibited the major labor federation, the Congress of South African Trade Unions (COSATU), from participating in any political action. Since March 1988, at least two newspapers have been suspended under emergency censorship laws that enable the government, without needing to take court action, to censor or close publications that it deems subversive. Stricter controls have also been placed on free-lance journalists and small news agencies, whose registration can be withdrawn if they are seen as posing a threat to public order. And in June 1988, following a three-day nationwide protest strike by more than one million black workers, the government announced the extension of the two-year-old state of emergency for another twelve months.

It would be wrong to assume that these events could in any way overturn or blunt the issues raised a year earlier in this symposium. If anything, they point to the validity of those issues, by demonstrating anew the forces that gave rise to them. The one constant in the lives of writers in South Africa is apartheid; it influences in some way every decision they reach about their work, and about the relevance and future of their varied literary culture itself. The vitality and commitment of the writers attending this conference make clear that

6

they will all persist in seeking expression and achievement, in spite of new restrictions and hindrances; they have done so throughout their lives.

The day after this symposium, a number of the participants also gave a reading of poetry and fiction at the Newberry Library in Chicago, which culminated in singing and dancing; and it seemed that, during the conference and reading, a miraculous window on South African literary culture had been opened here, half a world away from where the struggle to write and read is an everyday one, along with the struggle for freedom.

Reginald Gibbons and Fred Shafer
December 1988

"Man Going to Exile" / linocut by David Hlongwane.

OPENING REMARKS

Reginald Gibbons: I want to welcome you all here. I believe this is an historic occasion and I'm very happy that *TriQuarterly* and Northwestern could be a part of it and facilitate it. Although I don't claim to be an expert, I don't believe that any gathering like this has taken place before—certainly not in this area, and perhaps ever in this country. And I'm very happy and moved to see all the participants here.

I don't wish to take any time now except to say welcome to you and to tell you what we'll be doing. The president of the university, Arnold Weber, will offer some opening remarks for this conference; then we will have two panel discussions. I would like to invite Mr. Weber to come to the podium.

Arnold R. Weber: Thank you very much. I'm very pleased and honored to welcome you on behalf of Northwestern University. From the university's point of view this is a very important occasion. First, this conference is part of the university's continuing program of educating and sensitizing our community to the situation in South Africa and the grave injustices associated with the oppressive political and social system that currently exists in that country. The purpose of the programs that we have in the university is to keep our concern over conditions in South Africa before the university in a meaningful manner. We understand that this converence embraces both a literary and a political statement that reflects the fact that Northwestern, indeed, is part of a wider community and is passionately involved.

Second, we're very proud that the touchstone and organizing vehicle for this conference is a recent edition of *TriQuarterly, From South Africa. TriQuarterly* is the literary publication that's been put out by the university for twenty years. Over that period it has established a highly visible reputation for being venturesome and of high quality over the years. *TriQuarterly* has presented new literary modes, new dimensions

9

of criticism, and new authors of promise and achievement. So in a real sense this conference also affirms the stature of the university in a very important area of literature and literary criticism. *From South Africa*, I think is distinguished, as many reviews have indicated, by the fact that it presents a different set of observers and communicants. Everybody in this room is aware that the western view of South Africa through literature has largely been conveyed by white authors such as Alan Paton and Nadine Gordimer. This publication has been a vehicle for presenting the eloquence of many black authors who can offer more intimate insights into the South African experience.

And last, it's clear that beyond these political and institutional concerns the conference defines a literary experience. And it's a literary experience of great strength which really grows out of the power of simplicity. I recently read some commentary by Irving Howe, a well-known literary critic. In this commentary he cited a passage from T. S. Eliot which I thought was particularly apt for this occasion. Eliot said, "Great simplicity is only won by an intense moment or by years of intelligent effort, or both. It represents one of the most arduous conquests of the human spirit: the triumph of feeling and thought over the natural sins of language." It is that term, "the natural sins of language," which I think is startling but commands our attention.

I'm very glad that we as an institution, and through Reg Gibbons's leadership, can share in this triumph and act as the host for this event. I'm pleased to extend to you the full hospitality of Northwestern. Thank you.

Reginald Gibbons: Thank you very much, President Weber.

The first panel is on Fiction and Society in South Africa. These panels have been titled as loosely as possible to permit the participants to follow the direction of their own discussion, and it has seemed to me in the few minutes we've had together so far that it's going to be very important and most interesting for us as an audience to hear what they say *to each other* about the culture, the literature, the society and the political organization of their homeland, each from his or her own perspective. At this time I'd like to introduce the participants in alphabetical order. Daniel P. Kunene—scholar, writer of poetry and fiction–teaches at the University of Wisconsin, Madison; Njabulo S. Ndebele, an extraordinary and very prominent writer of fiction and literary criticism, has come from Lesotho; and Sheila Roberts, a fiction writer who teaches at the University of Wisconsin, Milwaukee. The drift of their remarks will be pursued by two respondents, who are the two guest co-editors of *From South Africa*, the two persons without whom none of this, much less the issue itself, would have been possible. They are David Bunn and Jane Taylor, who have also come from South Africa for this conference. I won't give extended introductions to them because you will find biographical sketches in the back of your program,* and with that I will turn the program over to Mr. Kunene, who will begin.

---

*See "Notes on Participants," beginning on page 122.

Fiction and Society in South Africa

Daniel P. Kunene, Njabulo S. Ndebele,
Sheila Roberts,
Jane Taylor, David Bunn

"Domestic Worker" / linocut by David Hlongwane.

Daniel P. Kunene: Many recent publications evaluating the literary scene in South Africa have demonstrated the diversity of literary genres, of themes, of writers' linguistic, cultural and social backgrounds, and of audiences that come out of that country. The most recent such publication is the special South African issue of *TriQuarterly.*

The South African writer daily has to make difficult decisions arising from these multiple choices: For whom should he write? What literary genre should he use? What particular theme seems most urgent at any given moment? What language must he employ? What cultural sophistication can he assume on his audience's part in terms of their ability to grasp the cultural nuances that come out of the story's milieu? Can a white audience whose social status exempts it from the horror daily experienced by black people fully grasp the sheer hell it is to live under those conditions?

Because of the diversity of languages in South Africa, the first and foremost problem some writers have to confront is that of language choice. This in turn suggests the problem of audience. A writer writing in Zulu like C. L. S. Nyembezi obviously has a Zulu audience in mind. Similarly a writer writing in Xhosa is targeting a Xhosa audience, a Tswana writer a Tswana audience, and so on. When Thomas Mofolo created the allegory *Moeti oa Bochabela*, he was speaking to the Basotho. Henry Masila Ndawo was having a Xhosa audience in mind when he created his hero Gqobhoka in *UHambo lukaGqobhoka*, and made him take a symbolic journey towards the adoption of the Christian faith.

Since the end of World War II and the ensuing "winds of change," the black people have sought to restore their own dignity and to take charge of their own destinies. They have sought to proclaim this new-found sense of liberation to the world. This is just one of many reasons why some blacks (relatively few in number by comparison) have decided to write in more widely spoken languages like English. In the South African context, on the other hand, there is a more urgent reason for adoption of English by some African writers: It is the desire to establish dialogue with the white oppressor and to force him to listen to the legitimate grievances and aspirations of the black people. But then there is always the inevitable contradiction that by thus speaking to a white audience, the black writer ironically becomes obscure to the bulk of his black brothers and sisters who have not been initiated into the mysteries of the white man's language. It is this bothersome problem that I tried to grapple with in my article "Language, Literature and the Struggle for Liberation in South Africa," published by *Staffrider* [Volume 6, Number 3, 1986].

The struggle for liberation in South Africa has reached a point where all these diverse audiences must be simultaneously addressed. A mighty challenge indeed! But there is a way out, and that is translation. Again, more recent collections of South African short fictions and poems have, on the whole, faced this problem by including African language pieces in translation. Translation must be given a high priority in South Africa. We have to face the fact that South Africa is a multilingual country with an urgent need for communication across language barriers. Literature specialists must link hands with comparative linguists of Southern African languages to come up with an efficient and economical plan for a massive translation project. Translation from one African language to another would benefit from careful linguistic planning, and this is where the linguist comes in. For example, to translate a piece of literature from Xhosa to Zulu, or vice versa, is extremely wasteful in time, energy and resources because of the high degree of mutual intelligibility between these two languages. A similar relationship exists between, for example, Sesotho and Setswana. Therefore an awareness of the grouping of the Southern African languages into the Nguni and

Sotho groups would help tremendously in making these determinations.

Then there is the problem of communciation between African-language-speaking and non-African-language-speaking writers. So far the solution to this problem has been a one-way stream. African-language-speaking writers who write in English have blazed the trail in facilitating this cross-cultural communication. In the process, some of these writers have exposed themselves to adverse criticism from the English-speaking group for their lack of adequate knowledge of English. Granted. But these same critics haven't taken even the tiniest step towards becoming proficient in at least one African language and thus contributing towards this cross-cultural communication. They *must* begin. If necessary, special private schools must be established for this purpose.

There are other formidable problems, however, facing the writer in South Africa. The law tells him what he may or may not say. This is not restricted to censorship laws, which indeed exist, but includes other so-called security legislation which restricts personal freedom. Laws that affect freedom of movement, freedom of assembly and association, and freedom of speech automatically also affect the writer's freedom to write what he thinks. This makes the writer an endangered species. He has to tread warily and say things without saying them. Here more than anywhere else, the reader has a grave responsibility, which is to complete the camouflaged or truncated messages the writer dares not make in an overt manner. As the writer's audience, the reader stands at the other end of the communication spectrum. Each individual reader completes the communication for himself or herself. It is a sign of maturity when he/she strives to *complete* the process in a sensitive way through asking the simple question *why*? Why does a young man from the rural areas who goes to find work in the city become a gambler, a thief, a fornicator who catches venereal disease, a gangster, a jailbird? Is it solely and simply because he is morally weak? Is he more easily corruptible than "normal" people? Or is it because the socio-political conditions blacks are subjected to in the cities are so bad that they could corrupt a saint? Why did he have to leave his home in the first place to find work in the cities? If the writer is assigning what we perceive to be the wrong reasons, it is our duty as critical and responsible readers to disagree with him/her, and assign what are, in our best judgment, the right reasons.

The crying need for the stark horror of South Africa to be made known to the world by, among others, the writers of fiction, is perhaps one of the most difficult challenges they have to face. The message forces its way to the foreground, catching the writer unawares. Where does reality end and fiction begin? Should we think of fiction and reality as two mutually exclusive and perhaps even warring entities? Is the writer condemned to being fictional at one time and journalistic at another, with the twain forever refusing to meet? The answer is an emphatic *no*. I think that one can say that the message is carried most powerfully and effectively when it and fiction are fully integrated. Fiction's success in making us cry or laugh or exclaim in wonder or love or hate can only be measured by the success with which it creates for us people with whom we can easily and naturally fall into relationships—that is, convincing characters with whom we can empathize. These become our friends and we hate to see them incarcerated, or they are the traitors who deserve their inglorious ends.

Be that as it may, the insistence of the message is sometimes too much, and the writer agrees to a compromise. Brian Bunting was moved by this to say, in a foreword to Alex La Guma's *And a Three-Fold Cord*, that "It is difficult to propound the cult of 'art for art's sake' in South Africa. Life presents problems with an insistence which cannot be ignored, and there can be few countries in the world where people, of all races and classes, are more deeply preoccupied with matters falling generally under the heading 'political'." [La Guma, *And a Three-Fold Cord*, Berlin: Seven Seas Publishers, 1964; Foreword by Brian Bunting, p.7.] Nadine Gordimer uses the term "testifiers" for writers who agree to give the message first place in their writings.

There are many such examples. The literature is used as a weapon of struggle in the war of liberation. One need only look in the pages of, for example, the earlier issues of *Staffrider* to see how anger spilled out of the mouths of children in poems and short narratives and descriptive pieces that sought to make the message as explicit as possible. It was in recognition of this writer's dilemma that James Matthews publicly declared that the first and foremost function of his poetry was to "record the anguish of the persecuted." He said:

> To label my utterings poetry
> and myself a poet
> would be as self-deluding
> as the planners of parallel development.
> I record the anguish of the persecuted
> whose words are whimpers of woe
> wrung from them by bestial laws.
> They stand one chained band
> silently asking one of the other
> will it never be the fire next time?

One consequence of this is that such writers combine fiction with exegetical statements. While, in many cases, this simply happens, in a few instances it seems to be done consciously. Mtutuzeli Matshoba in his *Call Me Not a Man* [Johannesburg: Ravan, 1979] quite intentionally engages in this movement back and forth between the fictional and the mini-essay mode in which he makes philosophical statements on topics dealing with the relationship of one human being to another.

Our discussion must also include the publisher as a kind of middleman who puts certain conditions to the writer. The latter is eventually pressured into a kind of self-censorship in order to meet the demands of his publisher.

Oral performances have come into vogue in the black ghettoes of South Africa for many reasons, including that of the quickness of dissemination, and the ability to capture audiences which, for a variety of reasons, might never get to read a message published as a book. There seems no doubt, however, that one of the greatest advantages of oral performance is that it eludes both the middleman, in the form of an unsympathetic publisher, and the censor.

The immediately contemporary writer in South Africa is of a young age. Indeed many writers, especially since 1976, the year of Soweto, are no more than teenagers. But this is in accord precisely with these children also being, in a brutally real sense, the warriors of the war of liberation. One is reminded of the Child Dragon Slayer, Senkatana, in one of the myths of the Basotho. Senkatana kills the Swallowing Monster, the Kholumolumo, which has swallowed all living beings except his own mother who was pregnant with him and escaped the Monster by pretending to be a lifeless object. In no time he grows from infant to warrior and goes to slay the Monster, and he releases all the people and animals trapped in this living tomb.

Sex barriers have also been significantly removed. The woman (the schoolgirl) is coming into her own as warrior/writer just like her comrade (the schoolboy).

The writer in contemporary South Africa faces formidable odds. Some of the writing will certainly not survive the period of its immediate relevance, namely the war of liberation. But the most urgent question right now seems to be the effective use of the literature as a weapon of struggle, rather than its ephemerality or permanence.

Njabulo S. Ndebele: I would like to first of all express my appreciation to *TriQuarterly* for having made it possible for us to come and share our experience of some of the problems of the written word with you in the particular context of South Africa. And notwithstanding jet lag, that is still very much with us, we will do our best to be as enthusiastic as possible in this matter.

What I'd like to talk about very briefly, in an attempt to highlight an area of particular interest to me, is the whole question of the relationship between storytelling and fictionality in South Africa. Whether there is a distinction or not is a matter that people can make their minds up about, but I'll begin from the assumption that there is a difference and that this difference has played an important role in the history of black South African literature. I begin from the premise that there has been a strong tradition of storytelling in South Africa, one that stretches way back. We have more storytelling than fictionality as a result, because the latter is an historically recent phenomenon. The storytelling has very long roots; in fact a few minutes ago through this wonderful evocation of the story of Senkatana and how he rescued the people there, we have heard a living example of this tradition. On the other hand we have the tradition of fictionality, which is relatively new and is in my view destined to play a very important role in the development of South African culture in general. This is because the movement of the South African revolution, I believe, is towards a greater institutionalization of science and the scientific attitude. This is inevitable because of the nature of the society that, as I will be talking about this afternoon, we are going to inherit: the complexity of it. In the context of this broad distinction, I would like to highlight the problem of the imagination.

It is my understanding that, regarding the storytelling tradition in South Africa, not as many demands have been made upon it as such, as have been made on fictionality. The reason is that the storytelling tradition, being somewhat informal, has partaken of a sense of self-confidence which is a feature of cultures that have an inherent sense of history. They can define, they can approach, the concept of universality through their own practical, indigenous experience: the storytelling tradition has been nourished by this sense of self-confidence. But the problem is that over the years, because of the nature of South African history, the storytelling tradition has not been accorded the official recognition that has been accorded to the tradition of fictionality—the implicit judgment here being that what is written is more important than what is spoken. That is the implicit judgment of history, the history of conquest, in South Africa.

But, nevertheless, because the storytelling tradition has been put in a kind of official limbo, demands were made on the written word to articulate the problems of modernity, specifically of oppression and the need for liberation. And precisely because of these demands, the area of interest, the area of focus, in the field of fictionality has been somewhat heavily restricted. And the dimensions of this restriction are defined to a very large extent by the demands of exposition such as we find in the world of journalism, such as we find in the writing of essays, in which the articulation of the need for freedom and justice is more direct. In that field, the field of direct exposition, the world of metaphor and language use is generally restricted and put in a subservient position to the message itself. And because the history of journalism has been at the forefront of this articulation of injustice and the need for freedom, and because of the very fact that the majority of our short stories in the English language were published in magazines, in newspapers, and so on, it has meant that the fictional tradition has developed very closely with the tradition of political exposition. So when many of our writers, the majority of them, take to the pen, they also want the story, the poem, to be as combative as the word of direct exposition.

This has meant that the social imaginative compass has somewhat been restricted. This, of course, is historically understandable. But I think the situation is now changing drastically because of the impact on the imagination of the changes currently taking place in South Africa. What we see is evidence of a reawakening which expresses itself in diverse forms—the most obvious of which, for example, is in the field of trade-union activity, in the field of general cultural mobilization, where we are aware, as we are going to have the testimony later on, of how culture, particularly growing from the storytelling tradition, is coming out of the factories of South Africa. We are aware also of the tremendous sense of struggle and optimism that is taking place in the townships—the creation of street committees, for example, as the single, smallest, most important democratic unit. The emergence of people's courts, the emergence of the concept of education, means that the search for alternatives has been broadened in such a way as to encompass the entirety of social cultural expression. And it means, therefore, that a new language, a language of struggle and optimism, is developing. It means that there is what one might refer to as a broadening of the social imagination, in which everything is being subjected to close scrutiny, and that new perceptions of the world around us are emerging, because we can see the end in view. The resulting sense of optimism is releasing the potentials of the imagination and is making the imagination fly in all kinds of directions.

Let me go back, then, to the question of storytelling and fictionality. The world of storytelling has never, in any manner, suffered from exactly the kind of restriction referred to earlier, because in that world people were free to be humorous, people were free to be satirical. They were free to take in the whole world without the anxiety of being politically irrelevant. The general society rather than politics as such was the framework of human interest. The world of storytelling is characterized by a broadminded self-confidence. And I think this self-confidence is beginning to invade, as it were, the world of fictionality also. And that in fact, for the world of fictionality to participate in this reawakening, it has to free itself of its limitations and draw from the world of storytelling so as to broaden the interest of the imagination. It means that the fiction of today should not and probably will not be afraid of experimenting with form, on the understanding that in South Africa to say that you cannot have art for art's sake will not mean anymore that you cannot have good art. In other words, the absence of the doctrine of art for art's sake does not mean the absence of good and socially relevant art. I think there is an increasing self-confidence that you can tell a story in as interesting a manner as possible—be interested in the form—without necessarily sacrificing a broader social and political interest. On the contrary, the more inventive you are, the more you are participating in, and adding to, this reawakening.

Perhaps I should give a different example here: take the situation where people—workers, for example—have been experiencing themselves as tools. You are in a factory, and all you have been doing is that you have been taught how to operate this machine. But you were not permitted to make suggestions about how you can make this machine perform better. I think that what is happening on the factory floors of South Africa is not only an interest in how the machine is working, but also in how the machine can be made, how it can be subjected to one's imagination—so that the machine itself can be part and parcel of a worker's expression of the new world around him or her. At a certain point, the politics governing the new relationship between the worker and the machine should give way to a tradition of invention. And as I said, this feeling is taking place in various ways, in various aspects of society. And it is bound to make an impact on the way we write our stories, on the way we plan a story, on the way we write our poems. And I think that tendency is well on its way and is going to gather momentum.

So what I'm really talking about here is the release of the imagination, in the context in which there is a confidence, a lack of fear of experimentation, a lack of fear of trying new things—because the world around you demands new things. It demands the opening of perception, the deepening up of perception, and the exploration of every avenue of society. And I think this is what is happening at the moment. In most of the stories, in *TriQuarterly #69*, the issue that has brought us here together, you will see this reflected. A shift away—but not an abandoning—a shift away from the overtly, as I say, political as such, a tactical shift away from it in order to accommodate the breadth of life and experience in South Africa. That new terrain of imaginative exploration has a direct impact on the way we imagine the possibilities of the future. That we can experiment with all kinds of forms means that society itself is ready to experiment with all kinds of ideas in the march towards an alternative future. And I hope that, as South Africans, this will be our single most important contribution to the world, the universal world of culture. It is beginning today and it is my understanding that it is likely to continue well into the future.

Perhaps in this regard, I should mention that writers—cultural workers—are organizing themselves today in South Africa, precisely with the view to equipping the author, the dramatist, the photographer, everybody, with the tools of the trade. Because the task before us demands that mastery. There can be no way back, there can be no concessions to that potential that is out there waiting to be opened up. I think I will stop there, at the moment.

Thank you.

Sheila Roberts: I'm going to limit my remarks to white South African writing in English. There are two points that I would like to make but that I'm making from a position of some ignorance, seeing that I've been living in the United States for the past ten years and have only had a few visits back to South Africa, and I could have a distorted vision.

The first point is that South African writing in English by whites—since 1948 with the publication of Alan Paton's book, *Cry the Beloved Country* [New York: Scribner's]—has kept in a kind of lockstep with political activity—not quite a lockstep as I read the writing through the fifties and sixties; it seems to me that what writers do in those decades is respond to what the government has already done. So that Gordimer's fiction, to cite one example, moves politically in response from her first book, *The Lying Days* [New York: Simon & Schuster, 1953], where what ideology infuses it is liberal, through to *Burger's Daughter* [New York: Viking] in 1979, where she is seriously having a character discuss communism as a viable political alternative.

She is responding, responding, to what is happening politically. But in the past few years, it seems to me what has happened with writers is that they have left the government and its various regulations behind and are projecting to a future that could or could not happen, or could happen or not happen the way they envisage it. So that in *July's People* [New York: Viking, 1981] Gordimer shows us the revolution already in action and white people fleeing the cities which are being bombed by the black fighters. In John Coetzee's book *Life & Times of Michael K* [New York: Viking, 1984], again he depicts the country in a state of revolutionary flux, with a movement of population. So what I'm saying is that, while previous writers have been one step behind government activity, two important white writers, at least, have stepped ahead and said, "This is what the future is going to be like."

But that brings one to the question of where do they go from there? They will have to then imagine a situation—postrevolutionary—and construct a society in which their characters can interact, one that is already, we hope, peaceful. The other thing that they could do, and which perhaps they are doing, is take a kind of refuge in fable or a rewriting of texts. John Coetzee's latest book, *Foe* [New York: Viking, 1987], shows us another possibility of Daniel Defoe's book *Robinson Crusoe*: that there was a woman on Crusoe's island and that she tries to get Defoe to write the story, but what she also wants is for Friday to tell his side of the story, except that Friday has no tongue. Of course, when Foe, as he's called in the book, writes the book we have, he leaves out the woman and he leaves out the black man's story. And so as I read Coetzee's book, I understand that he is saying you cannot tell the story without the woman and you cannot tell the story without having the black person's interpretation of history as well. So that's one direction that the South African white writer can go in.

Now the second point that I want to make very quickly is that in my observation, South Africans don't read their own literature. Any publisher there will tell you his sad tale of woes: nobody seems to make any profit. I'm surprised they keep going. I've just published my fourth book there and I can tell you sad stories of very tiny royalty payments. When I was there in August, I went to every bookstore I could and checked out what they carried, and they carried very few of the books I was looking for. I had to go to the publishers' offices or write for them. The people I spoke to hadn't read most recent South African publications. So I asked myself, why do South Africans not read their own writing— white South Africans? And I think the answer lies in an article that Christopher Hope wrote in which he describes South African white writing in English in this manner:

> The subjects are certainly large and important enough, but they are also aspects of one

central problem: race, the single issue which dominates our politics. And the result is a certain sameness, a predictability, a certain familiar ache in the heart of the South African novel which has become increasingly burdensome.

In other words, the ordinary South African person reading the literature written by South Africans is presented again and again in a very predictable manner with the same set of problems, the same set of horrors, the same sense of paralysis. But it's something, in various ways, people know and live with, so what they do if they read a South African, is they read the adventure stories of Wilbur Smith, and at least there is some escape. But South Africans must begin to read their literature and not only make it a financially viable proposition but also derive from it the kind of enjoyment people all over the world derive from their own literatures. And it's my sense that as this happens, as white South Africans simply write from the imaginative enjoyment of observing the world and the interaction of human beings, undaunted by this boring burden—clumsy, single-issue ideology–that the black writers will continue doing what they are doing currently and which my two colleagues have spoken to, and that is, create for their readership a sense of their own history and their own place as writers in the society.

Thank you.

Jane Taylor: I'm going to respond very informally and briefly and try and pick up one or two of the major motifs or issues that have been raised by the previous speakers. And I will just touch on these and leave it to David Bunn to clear up anything that I've left behind. So the first thing that I'd like to address is something raised by Professor Kunene, which I'm very pleased that he drew so much attention to. It became apparent as he spoke about Gordimer's allusion to testifiers, and as he also referred to James Matthews's comments that the poet was to record the anguish of the persecuted. It's quite interesting to look at this whole issue of the testifier in its context over the last forty years and also in its context currently today. Because it was so interesting for us in putting together the volume to see how that aspect of testimony was prevalent in a lot of the material that we were receiving.

In the last thirty or forty years, there has been a very strong emphasis on testimony, on the authentic voice of the authentic experience. So the almost unmediated experience of the victim of apartheid gave the work its legitimacy, to a certain extent, historically. And that is something that is still very prevalent today, that one sees in political meetings, in political organizations. Young people will testify: a space has been created socially for the testimonies of young people who are sharing their encounters, particularly the young detainees who have experienced the last ten years of crisis, really post-'76 (and ongoing, every second year or so, a kind of seasonal harassment will try and suppress the energies of the young in the community). The testimonial is something that is treasured as a valued artifact; and that is not something new.

What I want to emphasize is that it's actually feeding into a literary tradition, a tradition of writing about one's own experience. The autobiography is a very vital genre in the South African literary tradition, particularly with black writers. One of the interesting things that has taken place in the last couple of years is that black women writers in South Africa have started writing autobiographies, and it's interesting to consider to what extent they have been influenced by preceding writers, to what extent they're imitating the male form in choosing to write autobiographies. Someone like Ellen Kuzwayo, for instance, in *Call Me Woman* [London: Women's Press, 1985], is writing an autobiographical work, a clearly autobiographical work. Miriam Tlali is writing autobiographical novels to a large extent. Will that form—the autobiographical form, because of its associations with authenticity and so on— will that form stay the dominant form in black women's writing or will they find a different voice, something that still has to emerge? It's intriguing too because Kuzwayo, as well as a number of other writers, has received a certain amount of criticism for drawing attention to her own social and historical role in the autobiography. And of course this is a criticism that was never leveled at the male autobiographers. So that again raises an interesting question—why was Kuzwayo criticized? For assuming a male genre or for drawing attention to her role in an unfitting way?

The position of the black woman writer is a singularly difficult and complex one. I'd like to outline why it is a complex one. Obviously I am not speaking from my own experience, but as a female South African I have also grown up with a number of ideological constraints and pressures and it's something that one is constantly battling against. There's an interesting article by Carol Boyce Davies in which she cites a story from Noni Jabavu's *Drawn in Colour* [New York: St. Martin's Press, 1962], also an autobiographical novel, in which Jabavu describes how she and a friend who are dressed up to go shopping in town and need to go to the toilet, discover that there are two toilets for men, one for white men and one for black men, but there is only in fact a toilet for white women; there isn't a toilet for black women and the two of them have to go out into the bush. Davies does an interesting Lacanian analysis of how the black woman then is a double absence. She neither has the phallus—she is not male—nor is she white, in South Africa. Here's a kind of double negation of the existence of the black woman.

There have historically been a number of black women writers and it's going to be interesting to look and see what happens to the autobiographical form, whether it stays as dominant a form in black women's writing.

The other thing that I want to touch on is something that Sheila Roberts drew some attention to just now, and that was a new departure in South African writing. She was talking about the fabulous element that has developed in certain fiction and she cited in particular John Coetzee's *Foe*. This whole thrust is a very interesting one, and it's something that was really initiated by Coetzee in South Africa, although it's been inherited by certain writers like Menán du Plessis and Ingrid Scholtz, who is an Afrikaans writer but who does her own translating into English as well. They are theoretical writers to a large extent; their structures and their possibilities are not so determined by the kind of realistic autobiographical constraints that we were discussing earlier. Coetzee in particular is interested in investigating the issues of power and language and the structuring of the self inside ideology. So that affords the white writer a new way of speaking. Instead of being a liberal voice who can only empathize with the black situation but is never able to have claims to the authenticity of the experience, he gains an authority with which to analyze the power structures that actually determine the position of the white writer and of the black writer and of the white and of the black political participant in South Africa. That shift to a more theoretical and in some senses a more fabulous genre in South Africa is breaking new ground and making new generic opportunities available with the shift away from the liberal, dominant model that existed in South Africa for the last twenty or thirty years.

Those were just some of the main shifts that I wanted to outline, and David Bunn, I think, will pick, some of the others.

David Bunn: I'm afraid there's very little left for me to pick up. I think everyone around me has done such a wonderful job, and Jane has covered all the really exciting terrain, I don't know quite what to do about that. I'd like to just point to a few issues from our speakers' presentations that I think deserve highlighting and then I'm going to concentrate on two rather narrow areas.

First of all, I'd like to respond to something that Daniel Kunene said on the question of language which I think is a critical issue. It's also a question that Njabulo Ndebele has addressed quite extensively in *Tri-Quarterly*. The question of language is, of course, also the question of political struggle, in the sense that language in South Africa is obviously ideologically charged. All we have to do is think back on 1976 and how the language issue became such a determining thing in the streets. The question of Afrikaans was an ideologically charged issue which motivated people in their protests. But control over language is also part and parcel of apartheid's management procedures: the division of labor and the division of cultures is also reflected in the division of languages and the way languages are managed very specifically by the apartheid regime. (I'm just adding to the point that Daniel put very well.)

Also a quick response to the point that Daniel raised when he was talking about legislation and how the writer is, in fact, an endangered species: he mentioned that the reader in South Africa very often has to complete an incomplete text. This is a critical issue that we must discuss. Obviously, as editors it presented us with a particular problem in that it's very difficult to take an incomplete text and put it in a book. One of the things we did encounter, though—and I find this particularly challenging—is that it's often the actual legislative procedure that makes the incomplete text subversive. For instance, it's the definition of subversive statements in the Emergency Regulations that produces all sorts of subversive possibilities: spaces in newspapers—blank spaces—become potentially revolutionary. You remember that there was a moment in the Emergency Regulations—I think it was in 1985—when newspaper editors were prevented from actually leaving blank spaces to indicate where text had been edited out. That was seen also as potentially subversive. At one point there was even talk of banning the warning announcements in newspapers about how their coverage had been restricted. The strangest things, the most ephemeral things, can become subversive. And this is feeding the idea of the incomplete text Daniel was talking about.

Sheila Roberts focused on a point which we should perhaps discuss amongst ourselves: the—to use the phrase that she repeated from Christopher Hope—the "familiar ache of race" and how it appears in South African fiction. We should perhaps discuss the question of race as it is being represented in South African writing now, with particular regard to the material reality of South Africa, and organizations, and the discourse of race as it is manipulated by South African organizations. When Reginald Gibbons was organizing the conference, we had a very interesting conversation about a word that was to appear in the brochure. The word was "multiracial." And we had a debate about it. To South Africans, I think, and to South African audiences, the word "multiracial" has an appearance and a reality which you probably won't be aware of. "Multiracial" is associated precisely with apartheid's management procedures—the division between races and the whole "separate but equal" rhetoric that keeps apartheid in place. A more common word that would be used, I suppose, instead of "multiracial," is "nonracial." What does this mean about the presence of race and references to race within South African writing? To what extent has there been a shift away from "race" and towards an explanation in terms of class and state power?

Those are a few of the issues that occurred to me as I was listening to the speakers. I'd like to now focus on two narrow points. One relates quite specifically to what Njabulo Ndebele was saying. And I think it's best represented by the collaboration between storytelling and fictionality. I think eventually, Njabulo, when you were coming towards the end of your speech, you were talking about how the self-confidence in the story-telling tradition was now beginning to invade fictionality. And also fiction itself, I think you were suggesting, must actually draw on this world of storytelling—there should be more of an interpenetration between the sto-rytelling tradition and the terrain of fictionality. I would like to suggest that this is happening because of certain historical reasons in the South African context. If we just go back a bit we can look at the pressure that has been brought to bear on South African writers to present authentic experience—to represent suffering truthfully, for instance. Obviously one thinks particu-larly of the years of the 1970's, or beginning with the autobiographical tradition in the 1950's and '60's—but then in the 1970's, the concentration, especially through black consciousness ideology, on the idea of the authen-tic speaking of black identity. This has developed in a number of very interesting ways in recent years.

The perception, I think now in South Africa, is that there is a hegemonic or dominant ideology that must be opposed. And there is a considerable pressure on the novelist to act as a type of historian. Someone mentioned Mtutuzeli Matshoba's short stories. Mat-shoba himself is very conscious of his own role as a historian, of stepping outside of the novelist's position, taking on the role of the historian, and including a community. Ever since 1976 this tendency has been manifesting itself more and more. There's a commu-nity focus in the writing that wasn't there to the same extent previously. So if we look at South African cul-ture now, and South African fiction, there is a fullness, a fullness of tradition; there is a total engagement of the culture: it is not simply fiction, but it is fiction aware of the community, fiction aware of other art forms such as the praise poem and funeral oration. What Njabulo was referring to with this idea of interpenetration, I suppose, also expresses that fullness.

Secondly—and this is a very brief comment, again perhaps relating to something that was mentioned about writers and their actual political engagement and their organization—this to me is quite clear: if there is one movement in the past couple of years, it is a movement towards affiliation. There have been very significant shifts within the ranks of organizations in South Africa, organizations such as the UDF [United Democratic Front] and COSATU [Congress of South African Trade Unions] from specifically reactive positions—one thinks of the legislative and constitutional conditions that brought the UDF into being—to actually becoming formal structures with an autonomy of their own. The construction of separate governments within townships, the emphasis on people's power and people's education, the construction of alternative structures outside the dominant ideology—all of these focuses have had a particular bearing on the writing of fiction, and fiction in turn is often seen as contributing towards an alternative language of cultural liberation.

There is a notable emphasis with a number of fiction writers on the idea of affiliation—specific affiliation to specific organizations. A writer such as Menán du Plessis, for instance, is very much engaged with the UDF. In the past couple of months we've seen the formation of COSAW—a number of the people here were involved with that, the Congress of South African Writers. I think all fiction writers now, more than they were before, are expressing an emphasis on organizational affiliation. Now this has meant something rather strange, in a way. What I think has happened is that there is less of an emphasis, on the government's part, on the banning of novels and more of an emphasis on the affiliation of writers with political groups. So I don't think it's true to say, anymore, as André Brink has said, that South African writers are producing agitprop, which will then engage them in absolute struggle with the government. I really think the South African government is worried about writers who join organizations. This is reflected in the legislation of the past week, with the Universities Act, and the cracking down on intellectuals, and also perhaps with the Conor Cruise O'Brien affair—you may have heard of that—at the University of Cape Town and the whole debate about free speech.

Those are a few of my very rough ideas springing from the participants' actual presentations, but I think we should engage in questions now.

QUESTIONS AND ANSWERS:

[Questions posed without identification of the questioner are paraphrased or excerpted, below. The complete question-and-answer sessions are not reproduced here, for reasons of both space and poor audio recording.]

Question: Can you tell us more about how young black South Africans use people's courts and people's education?

Ndebele: Much that is negative has been said about people's courts, people's education and street committees. Much of it has come, of course, from antiresistance government propaganda. They have been charged with being instruments of organized violence, intimidation and indoctrination. All, of course, from the point of view of the state's aim of discrediting emergent and popular forms of democratic participation.

In reality, these emergent democratic institutions are genuine efforts at replacing oppressive apartheid institutions. Where they have been successful they have brought about a large measure of social cohesion and organized racial conduct in the townships. Obviously, at this point, being relatively new, they may still be very much at a low level of development. But they have a potential to be a viable alternative to the present forms of mass oppression.

One of the things that one can say immediately is that obviously these alternative grass-roots institutions have been the target of insistent opposition by the government in an attempt to stamp them out altogether. I think if most of us in here who are readers of the South African situation will be witnesses to the fact that some people who have actually been involved in some of these trials, in these courts, were brought to trial, and heavily sentenced. The idea, I think, is basically to stamp them out as far as possible. A similar situation occurs with regard to people's education. Because basically these are grass-roots organizations which are attempting to confront the state, not with rhetoric as such but by actually creating practical alternatives, practical civic institutions that will replace the institutions of apartheid. And one might possibly suggest that there has been a setback in this area, but I think the seed has been sown, and I think this is something that is likely to grow in the future. Similarly, the People's Education Project, which has a lot of broad-based support, has had its leadership under constant harassment. Most of them are in detention; some of them virtually live in a state of hiding all the time. So, practically, one would say that there are tremendous organizational problems, which we have to face; but I think that, as I said, the seed has been sown, and these are likely to be entrenched in the consciousness of people over a period of time. I can see them finding other ways of rearing their heads up once more.

The concept of people's education is organizationally symbolized or embodied in a national movement called the National Education Crisis Committee, which is the one that is organizing this project, which wants to realize this concept in practice. And I have already made reference to some of the difficulties. This enjoys a tremendous amount of support throughout the black community.

In the course of 1985, I think, young people came up with a slogan: "Liberation now; degrees later." This slogan occasioned much anxiety and controversy. However, the slogan, like all slogans of this nature, should really be understood in the context of the events out of which it emerged. I think it should be understood as the *mobilizing* slogan rather than that we have no need for education anymore. I think it should be understood in context; it was, at the time, a mobilizing device to focus our concerns on a particular problem—Bantu education, and the need for us all in South Africa to adopt a critical stance towards education and the manner in which education in South Africa has been institutionalized to the disadvantage of black people. But I don't think that it should be understood as meaning that there is no room for education; on the contrary—or we would not have a National Education Crisis Committee grappling with the issues of alternative education.

Kgositsile: I'd like to make a comment on the education thing—the Bantu education issue, the whole education crisis. It has to be understood in the context that, whether Bantu education existed or not, education in South Africa does not exist—any more than much of it exists in this country, for that matter. O.K.? I just want that to be clarified, from the very beginning.

But there are a few things in connection with fiction which have been said which puzzle me very seriously— give me problems. There is the question, for instance, of storytelling and fictionality. I do not understand the demarcation line. What I mean is, even if you were talking about fantasy, even if you were talking about mermaids or things like that, anyone's imagination is rooted in reality, to start with. If you were going to create a monster, with the head of a buffalo, the hooves of some other animal, a woman's huge boobs, a tail of a cat, all of that, what might make that fantastic fictional storytelling is that those things exist in reality, all of them exist, but they do not exist in that kind of relationship. So whether you are storytelling or whether you are fantasizing or fictionalizing, it seems to me basically if your imagination is healthy you are doing the same thing.

Ndebele: I'm glad that my colleague Kgositsile has asked the question, requesting to have a clarification, because obviously he has misunderstood what I was trying to say. Basically I am referring to the context of storytelling; I make the distinction between storytelling and fictionality in the context of one being a tradition basically oral in nature and the other being a matter of the written word. The way in which people are socialized into storytelling is largely informal, historical, community-based. I learnt many folktales in the context of the family—stories being told by my grandmother, and we competed in the business of storytelling among ourselves. I'm making reference basically to an informal cultural practice which over the years has been sustained in the context of the family. When I'm talking about storytelling I'm talking about people in buses, in trains, everywhere, at the corners of streets—gathered there and talking about the day—telling stories of all kinds. And I'm trying to suggest that the range of interests in this context of storytelling has been very, very broad and continues to be so even today. What distinguishes the storytelling tradition from the tradition of fictionality in the context of the history of black South African fiction is the abiding human interest that you find there in the former—that basically is it. The range of interests is very, very broad. And I think it is germane at this point to refer to the situation with regard to fiction writing in the indigenous languages. There the human interest has remained broad, but this has not been the case as far as fiction writing in English has been concerned. Because the fiction writing in English has been very much a battlefront fiction. Fiction in the indigenous languages has been very much under the control of the system—publications for the school, for example; the publishing situation there is dominated by the Afrikaner publishing houses and various church interests. By and large, with many notable exceptions, the human interest is very broad, but not as politically engaged, in many ways, as fiction writing in English.

So what I'm talking about is that fiction writing is a technique of writing that is attached to, that is developed in, formal institutions of education. To know how to write, and read, is a conscious act of education. And to master the tradition of fictionalizing, in the written word, involves mastering, being exposed to, the history of fiction writing, in the same way that in the tradition of storytelling you learn within that tradition itself. So I think the distinction is there, and maybe one can even use a very simple example here—that when I speak I have a lot of freedom to use my voice, to use my facial expression, to use my hands, which is not there when I am writing. The business of writing is inherently different from the business of speaking, and if you move from that premise, then you arrive at different art forms that have a lot in common that they share, but basically the approach to the use of those forms is very different.

Question: How does trade unionism act as a catalyst to connect storytelling and fictionality?

Ndebele: The panel this afternoon, I presume, will be dealing specifically with this issue, so maybe you want to be there. From my perspective, what I was trying to point to is that within the trade-union movement, as we will hear this afternoon, there is a concerted cultural activity—very self-conscious. People who previously had no voice—because literature was defined very narrowly as the English novel, poetry was defined very narrowly as English poetry—suddenly you find people now in the factories, most basically workers, with a worker background, who have found a voice in the context of the emerging political activism in the country. What they have to say is important, has always been important, but is now assuming even greater importance because it is taking place within the context of organized political activity. And it is this that is happening, which we are going to get more details about, later today.

Question: I'm not sure what the purpose of fiction writing is—to change the culture? I guess it is. What can you say after we have had *Cry the Beloved Country*?

You can write it five hundred different ways and it still comes out the same. The white South African doesn't particularly want to read any more because he's tired at ten at night. Perhaps ten percent of the whites recognize something's got to be changed, and they want to change, but you've got eleven tribes; what can happen if you've got eleven tribes, all speaking eleven different languages? Every tribe has its own purposes, and they want to be the king or the head of the blacks. What can you realistically do about it? Because I think that the white South African—he doesn't want socialism; anyone who's got property doesn't want it taken away.

Roberts: That is a dilemma that perhaps we could talk about afterwards. What the confusion here is, is what a reader expects from fiction, from a novel, from an artistic experience or a literary experience. And because South African literature has been focusing on this problem in a kind of repetitive way, readers are looking for something fresh. But what I'm talking about is, Why do we read? What do we expect? We expect a certain kind of pleasure, a certain kind of freshness. And what the South African novel has to do if it wants to have South Africans read it, is get beyond the same old churning out of problems. But I think we have no more time for this particular discussion.

D. P. Kunene: I want to respond to one of several rather startling, strange statements made by the last questioner. I would like to know—maybe I shouldn't say I would like to know, but I am surprised, I'm wondering where the questioner gets his information about tribes—"eleven tribes." You see, this is the kind of thing that the South African government is feeding people outside all the time, saying that there are tribes who are warring, who have to be separated all the time. That is why you have your "bush colleges," one for Xhosa, one for Zulu, one for Basotho, and so on, and you have Bantu homelands, which are not working precisely because they are based on false premises. And so I just have to express my surprise that you don't seem to have marched with the times—that what you are saying isn't at all in accordance with the facts.

Question: Given what Daniel Kunene just said, do South African writers strive to address this flow of misinformation or disinformation or misconceptions which comes out of the country and is received outside it? Is that an issue for South African writers?

D. P. Kunene: First of all, about the issue of trying to write something to entertain—I believe everybody would agree, we'd like to read a book that entertains us—but apart from that, on the issue of the political situation, the relevant issues, in South Africa, I would say that writers who are conscious of applying themselves to these, don't necessarily select one thing as against another. They do sometimes, let's say in a short story—I'm thinking again of Mtutuzeli Matshoba—pick up one of those things, it is true: for example, "Three Days in the Land of a Dying Illusion" details how the first-person narrator in the story visits the Transkei after it's declared so-called "independent" under Matanzima. Another story, "A Pilgrimage to the Isle of Makana," a visit of the speaker of the story to his younger brother, who is incarcerated on Robben Island, and so on. And so I suppose the answer to your question is, "Yes, they do"—without saying "We are trying to disabuse those who don't know or those who refuse to know of their fantasies of the South African situation by simply talking about it in those terms." There's a lot of different things that Matshoba does in his book—"A Glimpse of Slavery," a story detailing how three young black men are arrested on technical things, like the pass not being right, and one of them has just fought with a white co-worker. They are taken to a Boer's farm, where they are virtually slaves. So really, I think the answer is yes, the writers do address those issues.

Roberts: Could I add to that? I don't want you to get the suggestion from me that writing should simply entertain and be a pleasurable activity without a serious social concern. I'm making a distinction between white writing and black writing. And as someone pointed out, the white writer can only sympathize with the black suffering, and that is where the repetition comes. The white writer isn't in that situation of suffering, and it seems to me we've come to where white writers have stated and restated that sympathy or empathy. The black writers—it's their business to fight this battle and fight it through their literature. Another point I'd like to make is that there is writing that is not necessarily fiction—essays and other forms can also clarify for the outside world what's happening there.

Poetry and Society in South Africa

Mazisi Kunene, Ingrid de Kok,
Alfred Temba Qabula,
Keorapetse Kgositsile, Anne McClintock,
Neville Choonoo

Woodcut by Cecil Skotnes.

Mazizi Kunene: I must confess that, in a way, I come from a rather different perspective, because I write in an African language. I think that the act of writing in African languages has got its own dimensions—i.e., the direction in which the poetry, or the literature in general, develops. I think my colleague Mr. Ndebele indicated that there is a difference in the direction which is taken by literature written in the African tradition and the Anglo-African fiction written in English. He stole a lot of my thunder about things I was going to say, in dealing with characteristics that make these two strategies different. On the one hand we are concerned with a statement that is relevant to the present, in terms of the politics that, as Professor Dan Kunene also indicated, addresses the oppressor. That statement *has* to be in the English language because it is this language which the oppressor understands. As this statement is being utilized, projected, it also modifies the thinking or the mentality of the writer, because, as he creates, he is aware of the audience which is foreign—i.e., not his own. It is therefore not only to the audience of the oppressor which the author addresses, but that of his own people, at least those who can understand the English language. So in this conflict we have a popular combative literature that is written in English—a literature too which explicitly states the idiom of struggle. However, we must remember that words are not weapons.

It is not quite accurate, of course, to say that the literature that is written by Africans in their own languages is not combative. It is a question of difference in approach and a different style. The style of African traditional literature is complex. It is based on a diverse system of symbols on indirect statements that focus on the concrete experience. In the African literary idiom one is operating on two levels: one that is fictional and the other that is realistic. The former reorganizes the material and attempts to make the symbols meaningful to a large body of people. On the other hand, there is a deeper level that must be understood by those who are exposed to the experience as defined by the philosophy of the society. It is very important, I think, to understand these differences. When one chooses the fabulous forms, as Coetzee has done, one actually applies the techniques that are closest to African traditional forms of representation, in which case one is not so concerned with the fictitional aspect as with reality. However, one too has to elaborate on the literature in such a way that there is a level at which the ordinary person can focus on the entertainment part of literature while at the same time a more intelligent and reflective person can make an interpretation based on a much deeper level of meaning.

Much of the literature that is written by Africans in African languages does not explicitly state its combative intention, but uses the indirect form. This is more effective since it caricatures those who are in power. They are made to look ridiculous in a literature that lampoons them and follows with a restatement of the value system which, in effect, says, "Our traditions, our value systems, our institutions are superior." That in itself is enough, as a combative posture, to challenge those who have claimed that their institutions are better. But for many who do not understand the African languages, of course, this is always very difficult to grasp; it's always very difficult to penetrate because the meaning is, as I say, hidden.

African poetry in particular must take into account the existence of a wider audience. It also has to take into account the deeper intentions of the African ethic. African literature is no literature unless it is used as a vehicle of ideas. In it there is no elevation of the element of entertainment. African literature is concerned with the observation of the world-order as defined by African cosmology. Even at the level of children it is not concerned necessarily with the story, but with adult social actions which are defined as either desirable or undesirable according to the conclusions of the text. In examining African literature in African languages, one has no choice between being in society and being literature. Literature is inevitably bound up with social action. This is the very essence of African literature. I think the idea of an elitist literature itself originated from Western segmentation between society and literature or between literature and social drama.

It is logical, therefore, that the people who are workers in the mines and everywhere have begun to revive traditions of their own literature. The revival is not merely because it is fashionable to do so. But the revival is precisely because they have suddenly got the confidence, as somebody pointed out, the confidence that, yes, our institutions have got a validity of their own. Our institutions are even superior to the institutions of the foreigner. Our literature in its form, in its esthetic strategies, in its social strategies, is superior to that which is merely private, that which merely elevates a private fantasy. I think in that context one of the problems of South African literature written in English is its excessive focus on situations without reference to an ethical center. Consequently, literature written by white South African authors is often boring—i.e., descriptive without a universality of meaning. In this sense the writer exposes himself/herself as quite mediocre, projects not characterization, but a situation which he/she either says he/she agrees with or does not agree with. This is not to say all writers are writing in this form—I think Coetzee is one of the few people who has really attempted to deal with characterization, with the separation of individual incidents, and analyze them and project them through characterization on a universal scale. There are, of course, other authors who have tried to do that in the past. But on the whole, the predominance of the biographical material in South African white literature means that there is a tendency to reproduce the photographic experience or philosophize on it and not to elaborate on it imaginatively. So although this literature is concerned with the serious problems of social origin—like race, apartheid—it falls far short in scope to the demands of this internationally significant material. I think those Africans who write in English, indeed as Professor Ndebele himself indicated, are trying to elaborate on these elements to make their literature more universally meaningful.

The problem is a vast one, and it is very difficult to begin to deal with all its varied aspects, but these are just some of the hints on what I think is happening, that in the future the greatest literature that will emerge from South Africa will be a literature written by Africans in African languages; in fact, I am sure of it. It is they who have faced the tensions of having to redefine their history, redefine their meaning of the world in which they live, and redefine the world which has been distorted by occupation. That doesn't mean that this redefinition excludes; it never has excluded; the vision of the African world has never been exclusive, it has always been inclusive. It is, I think, logical, therefore, to ask for the participation, at least in terms of the content of the vision, of the white writers, of the other writers, in this perception. But I think the dynamics of African literature in African languages is going to take the lead. It is going to take over the mobilization of the general populace of South Africa and provide the necessary cultural hegemony on a universal scope—on condition, of course, that it creates a higher vision than the vision that has been presented by the literature, the social structure, the political structure, that we have hitherto experienced. And I think it has got this great possibility of coming out with a new idiom, a new dynamic idiom, and a new vision. South Africa, with its long history of regionalism, nationalism and racism, has a lot to contribute. In other words, literature has to be even more combative in future than the confrontational literature of the current era of apartheid.

Thank you.

Ingrid de Kok: I shall be addressing only one very small aspect of the large and challenging topic of *Poetry and Society in South Africa,* which we are to discuss today. I am concerned to raise a few questions related to the production of predominantly *lyrical* poetry, predominantly as *written* text, and in the necessarily limited context therefore of a very small segment of South African society—that group which is literate, and even smaller, almost nonexistent: that group which reads English poetry. By "written" I mean poems which are written primarily for publication, although they may also be performed. My emphasis is not because I consider this form of literary production or this genre or this privileged group of imaginary readers to be a particularly significant force in the development of a national culture; there are other people here much more equipped than I am to address the meaning of the development of workers' poetry in a country which must ultimately submit itself to working-class leadership. In some ways I think that is the poetry deserving the most attention.

There are also others here who can talk about the poetry being read and sung at funerals and at cultural rallies throughout the country. I have performed at some of those but I do it very poorly, and I am only able really to talk about that smaller—historically rather beleaguered—object, the personal lyric. I am also obviously speaking within the context of my class, my color and my gender, and they all determine what I will say about the lyric.

Jane Taylor and David Bunn mention in the Introduction to *TriQuarterly* that it's hard to resist the idea in South Africa that there are only two kinds of texts: those that make a daily difference and those that don't. I don't think the lyric makes a daily difference; I do think it makes a sort of a difference in some contexts, sometimes. And because it's what I do, I am inclined to argue for its development. Beyond that, the problems that are associated with this particularly individualistic form of writing may be of interest to anyone debating the issue of a people's literature.

There are three aspects about the production of lyric that particularly interest me at this time in South Africa.

The first is the question—which is a general question not specific to poetry, and I think has been debated here already—of legitimacy. The question of, who am I that I may write in South Africa? What may I write, what may I not write? Why should I write at all? The second question is the question of influence and role models—whether it's possible to write a *South African* lyric, whether it's possible for there to be such an object. What makes one a South African poet and is there only one way to be that? And a third thing that concerns me is—considering the fact that poetry is potentially the densest and most subversive form of linguistic expression—why is it that there are so few women poets in South Africa writing in English? (Almost none writing in English, though many writing in Afrikaans, however.)

To turn just very briefly to the question of accountability/legitimacy—it is one of the contexts within which one has to speak about one's own writing and that of others. It has been mentioned here today that, as repression has taken its toll of political organizations, the cultural arena has been given more attention by those in the progressive movement to help develop a sense of unity and national purpose, and to articulate the needs, views and voices in the land. But it is apparent that this is a secondary, alternative strategy intended to consolidate gains, keep issues alive, draw people together, in the absence of directly political opportunities.

Most practices in the cultural sphere of necessity therefore constellate around the large and compelling inevitability of national liberation, and are a part of the preparation for that day. Those who write poetry are thus, like other cultural workers, required to declare themselves. And it's not surprising that in a country where the word is an agency of legislation, where it's a lie, a fiction, a renaming, a distortion, where it's owned by the state, that the legitimate political opposition often appears to distrust the word and only trusts action.

This is a country, after all, where we preface "so-called" before many of the appellations we apply to each other. The state calls people "white" and "colored," and progressive people will say "so-called white," even using fingers in the air to signal the quotation marks. It's the country of the "so-called," and calling is therefore very important: what one calls or names is crucial. To call correctly, to use the correct political language—not to say "multiracial," but to say "nonracial"—has sometimes been a matter of life and death for people.

In other words, it's impossible to write poetry in South Africa without confronting the experience people have had of language: the expectations they therefore have of the word and of writers, whose ambiguous function is to undo the word while using the word.

These are expectations born out of an intense struggle in an environment which is often hostile and suspicious of ambiguity. Since this after all is one of the vital resources of the lyric, the poem is subject to deep suspicion: its ambiguity might just be a cover for liberal doublespeak. This environment is often anti-intellectual in aspect (for the ruling class has traditionally owned the means of intellectual production), and it's often hostile to those whose progressive declarations in their work have not been tested in the crucible of political activity itself. There are several problems associated with this, one of which is that the expectation can often conflate competence with commitment, with credibility: in other words, only someone who has political legitimacy has something worth saying. If the political commitment is judged good, the writing, no matter of what quality, may be valued likewise. On the other hand, while the problems associated with this are legion, it is what's, after all, a transitional and prerevolutionary phase, and there are prescriptions which, I think, have to be respected. One is, after all, confronted much more directly than most poets in most countries with some of the questions that perhaps all poets should be asked: the questions within the context of my class, gender and color—why do I write, what may I write and what do I write for?

What seems to me to have happened amongst some poets who have been struggling with these questions is that they have defected (although perhaps that's not the word I should use) to the ranks of political or cultural organizations. Or they have participated in poetry only as a kind of adjunct to their political work. Another option taken by a group of potentially talented English-speaking poets has been to retreat into a transparent cocoon of world-weariness, insisting on their intellectual connections with a profoundly conservative European tradition and decrying what they feel is a drop in standards. Another option is to try to write according to the prescriptions and themes that one perceives to be approved; that is particularly fraught with dangers, because it can produce a set of registers that are just reaction, defiance and assertion. And of course a national culture needs more than these registers, as well as a healthy dose of internal criticism. But that is changing too, and I think *TriQuarterly* demonstrates that those registers have changed quite considerably in the last little while.

For the moment, it seems to me, the written lyric must take account of its historical context and be seen to be doing so. And that accounting in itself must make it political. For political it must be. Not in any simplistic or singular way. But it means that the traditional features associated with the lyric, things like reflection and irony and analysis, must be put to the service of the historical moment in all its urgency. It may be then possible for it to make a minor contribution, if not a daily difference.

The second thing that interests me is the question of influence. What makes one a South African poet, if one is not a performance poet, or a worker poet? Quite apart from the challenging experience of writing at this most important time in South African history, I think the lyrical poet has a unique opportunity to unlearn some of her or his assumptions about the form and to refresh and toughen—and potentially even South-Africanize—the lyric. As it's commonly received in South Africa, the lyric is still English property, part of our colonial inheritance. And any white poet or black poet with my educational class background will have been exposed to predominantly English models, and some North American influence. The conscious accessing of South American or European poetry is much more recent for most of us. The question that has to grip one is: how can one be South African, how can one integrate, say, the influence of the Romantic tradition with the influence of, say Carolyn Forché or Derek Walcott, Galway Kinnell or Margaret Atwood, and then subject these influences to the challenges, say, of performance poetry and the older tradition of praise poetry about which people like me know almost nothing?

While it is still premature to comment on trends, what is beginning to be noticeable in a small way is the degree to which poetry published recently is absorbing the lessons, for instance, of performance poetry. Some of the energy generated by the knowledge that there are people out there who want to participate in the development of a new language has strengthened the poetic discourse. And some white poets are beginning to write with a louder voice, utilizing a larger rhetoric. The post-colonial lyric voice has to lose its faltering and minor, somewhat secretly self-aggrandizing, tone, to adopt a braver more assured register and to take risks, to own opinions, views and visions—not to play hide and seek with them. All of us are learning from performance poetry, from its most effective practices—repetitions, alternating voices, and lists of the dead, of martyrs, heroes, places of suffering and triumph. These practices can help concretize subjects that too often have

been left vague and generalized and therefore historically unspecific and safe. There are also signs that the
admixture of languages that one sees in performance
pieces, songs and rallies, is entering the English lyric,
hitherto so pristine. And it seems to me that for people
like myself one's personal project has to be to become
trilingual.

Finally, the practice of performing one's poetry can
revitalize one's work. There's nothing quite so chasten-
ing as performing before two or three thousand
people—when you have been trained to whisper your
poetry to you yourself or pretend you have a Richard
Burton baritone—and actually encounter a real audience
that responds and sometimes doesn't like what it hears.

Of course, there are lots of traps, and much of what
is being performed is dreary and repetitive. It's not
difficult to plug into tried-and-true formulas, to invoke
a mother here, a child there, a list of the fallen here, a
Casspir there, attempting a heroic tone. That kind of
exploitative reworking, especially (but not only) when
done by people who have not experienced the repression that they are reflecting—that sort of exploitative
reworking does discredit to what is the mass of meaning of such symbols in a country like South Africa.
Finally, what can sometimes be devalued as "occasional
poetry"—the sort of poet-laureate stuff that is written
under direction and sanitizes events—can have its value
restored in South Africa. One thinks particularly of the
work of Jeremy Cronin and others here—poets who have
charged their poetry with a consciousness of the Historic Occasion. The lyric in South Africa, whether occasional, or elegiac, or celebratory, or anything else, may
stand ready to be revitalized.

The third aspect I wish to consider is one I am
personally quite preoccupied with—the question of why
there are so few women writing poetry in English in
South Africa. Where are the female perspectives that
are found, say, in Canadian poetry? This dearth is reflected in *TriQuarterly* itself, where most of the poetry

written by women is by Afrikaans women; and I think this is a fair reflection of the state of the art in the country. At one level, it's not, of course, at all surprising: the South African state itself is so overtly male in its self-conception, representation and control, that it's understandable that women are still silenced, absenced. Except that doesn't explain why there are many women writing in Afrikaans.

More problematically—and I know this a rather tabooed subject—amongst the liberation movement there's an assumption that sexism is an invention of colonialism and that a postrevolutionary South Africa will automatically uproot sexist attitudes and practices. I'm simplifying, of course; some attention has been given to those issues in progressive groupings in the country. But the work is still very sporadic. Antisexism is part of the platform of most democratic groupings, and there have been developments recently within the UDF [United Democratic Front] and other organizations which should do much to reintroduce South Africans to the female leaders of the past, who through great personal sacrifices made lasting contributions to the struggle. And there are self-initiated groups in the Western Cape, and no doubt elsewhere, in which people are studying the position of women in revolutionary change. But still, on the whole, women are silent or silenced. And women who raise the question are often accused of divisiveness, of weakening the impetus and struggle.

South Africa is so deeply phallocentric, it seems to me, both in its present capitalistic and racist mode, and in the practices of its progressive opposition, that these dismissals need constant confronting. For some women, in some situations, this has required great courage. The contribution of women is under-researched, mystified or romanticized. A particular feature of the political struggle is the cult that surrounds the wives and widows of imprisoned or killed political leaders. While one has great respect for the women involved, it is telling that it is generally only as wife, daughter or mother of

Africa that women are accorded significance. I recently heard a prominent woman of great political influence express the view that feminism was a dangerous import and that it was the role of women to be "the bearers of the future citizens of South Africa." This echo horrified me, because when I was twelve I heard a Dutch Reformed minister say to a group of adolescent Afrikaans girls that "You are the future mothers of the future sons of South Africa." The double absence that Jane Taylor spoke of seems to me at work here: women as transmitters of the male culture, doubly disfigured.

No wonder women don't write. Many of you will be familiar with the way women have figured in South African prose; they don't figure much at all in South African poetry in English. They're scarcely there. One reason may be that there are few models used to help us with reformulating the position of women. South Africa has its own historical amnesia, partly a result of state control, and it is also deeply xenophobic. What could we learn from the role of women, for instance, in the revolutionary phase in Algeria, and of their fate afterwards, or about women in Cuba? Without these contexts, women in South Africa cannot speak of the female perspective or the woman's voice, lest they seem to have fallen prey to a particularly discredited North American bourgeois influence. We need to develop a more politically sensitive understanding of women so as to become more historically responsive.

There is, I think, enormous scope for a poetry to develop which investigates and honors those women who have been and continue to be resistant and creative, and those women who've told stories and made history, and which can re-evaluate existing political, social and philosophical values. To speak as a woman is to enter a role even more intersected with questions of authority, audience, modes of production, than those who speak politically as committed men poets. But it's not enough to uncover old heroines or imagine new ones. There have to be new forms as well.

To write poetry is to engage with prevailing forms of language, but I'm not suggesting that women are trapped forever within a male discourse, that language is inherently male. In a country that's reconstructing itself, with great labor, the opportunity to assert the importance of women's experience "to sieze speech" is there. The word is especially disqualified in South Africa; how much more available then is it for reworking by women? To have as one's endeavor the definition of the female self is one thing; to be defining within the context of a fractured state and revolutionary pressure is quite another. For what sort of revolution is worth fighting for that perpetuates myths which exclude half its comrades? The female knowledge of the female experience encoded in poetry cannot but be useful for post-revolutionary South Africa. I'm not talking of a separate-but-equal language, but of an inclusive one, and women in South Africa are particularly placed to disassemble, to reassemble and interpret, to reimagine, the self. This work could help in a small way to reconstitute a fuller story of our internal life and of our history, not the partial one we still privilege as "true," as "real."

Thank you.

Alfred Temba Qabula: [Qabula spoke extempora-
neously in Zulu, and bit by bit his presentation was
translated by Mazisi Kunene. Italicized comments are
interjections by the translator while in the act of translating.]

[In English:] I'd like to thank the *TriQuarterly* to
invite me to come here. It is very nice to see the other
side of the face of the moon. So, by that, I'm very sorry, because I have to stand, or to go back to, Zulu language.

[Translated from the Zulu by Mazisi Kunene:]

Hard to translate. My name is the son of so-and-
so, and so-and-so, and so-and-so, and so-and-so, who was
never afraid.

I'm coming from Flagstaff in Pondoland, where
my ancestors are buried. And where my forefathers and
us have seen all our wealth being taken away.
The capitalists forced us to leave our homes, to go and
work as contract laborers in Johannesburg. My father,
my own father, worked in the mines in order to feed his
own children.

After that I too had to go to Johannesburg and work
there after joining the resistance in order to stop the
demarcation of our land, the cutting down, cutting up of
our land.

Twenty-two years I worked for Dunlop Company,
exploited by a company called Dunlop, Dunlop Tire Company, that makes tires.

Imagine that! We were making the tires for cars
that we never owned, for all the Saracen tanks that went
chasing our children all over and us, the police cars,
and everything. It was us who were making these tires.

I was so mad as I was driving a truck at Dunlop
that I would feel so angry that I would make everybody
in the street, including those in my factory, to go almost
insane with anger, because I was underpaid, I knew all
the time that I was paid very little.

I worked hard, dust everywhere and fumes of
carbon, absorbing fumes into my system like other

workers too, who were as unprivileged as I was, and all this I did in order to survive.

Imagine that. This owner of the factory I worked so hard for got all the money and I only got a little bit, a very, very small amount—just leftovers. *Shame!*

As I worked in this factory, day and night, I got some chance, sometimes, to compose poems and songs on my fork-lift, and these poems—poems and songs—were about the experiences that I and other workers were going through in this firm, in the community and in the countryside.

Soon as we decided, we came together as members of a union and we decided to create directions and guidelines, which we wanted to make available to other workers, so that like us they also in turn should organize in the factories. Then I started writing. It was at this time that I wrote a poem that got me into a lot of trouble, the police asking me questions and various things about what I had written.

They would ask me whether I'd been to university, but I told them, "I have not been to university myself, but I've been to a higher and a better university." University of life in the factory, in the hostel where I was living under terrible conditions, in the country where I worked, in the mines; this was my greatest university.

I wrote, I created these poems, and also asked the others, encouraged others, to make these poems, and to perform these poems during the many meetings that we held as workers in the factory. I was the founder of this movement.

All this we did as a community, solid community together, there was nobody who was a superior or was inferior. No higher head of the union or lower head of the union. We did it as a team, as a group together, and we projected this idea to other people also to follow up in the same way, to create similar organizations.

This we did in order to communicate, firstly, our feelings of anger, and to communicate also our desires and ideals of a free South Africa, not the South Africa of slavery and oppression.

And now we have many such performances of poetry in various factories in Natal, in parts of South Africa, the Transvaal, and so on, that have copied this method of communicating our ideas, our own anger, our own suffering, so that everybody knows about our situation. And we are very strong in this technique, so much so that in every meeting of the workers you must be sure that there will be a person who has composed a song about what has happened or composed a poem or poems about what has happened and what should happen. So we use culture as a way of mobilizing and as a way of projecting our own ideas of a free South Africa.

We have now created a formal organization of workers in order to stimulate this cultural awakening and to enable others who have got talent to participate and elaborate on this form of projecting political ideas and visions. So this is the most efficient method we've found of communicating our ideas to others, even those who cannot read—others who can experience, who can articulate their experiences—and we find that we have a large number of people who are participating in this general message of liberation and freedom.

I must say, in the end—*of course English is so weak!*—I must say that things are changing, and they'll continue to change, and we shall be triumphant in the end. Amandla!

Keorapetse Kgositsile: This will probably be the shortest speech—and I'm not trying to make it proportional to my height. But there are a number of things that disturbed me a little bit. I thought that, supposedly, as writers, we talk very, very openly, cut out the pseudo-academic, pseudo-intellectual, whatever whatever, and just address ourselves to life, as South African writers. Especially if what gives any validity or authority to our writing is any inkling of a sense of responsibility to affirm life as creative activity.

And outside of the politeness, I think there are certain dishonesties; I don't want to get into details about that, but that disturbs me. I just want to register that, simply. Also, I do not think there is anything unique about the South African writer—black or white—that is different from literary tradition anywhere on this planet. And we do not have to be apologetic about the themes that preoccupy us, about the forms we use—techniques, styles, whatever. No apologies about that. The point is that, no matter what our egos might be, if we are talking specifically about black writers in South Africa, and we talk about those who write predominantly in English, like me, those are, in terms of the literatures of South Africa, an insignificant minority. It has always been that way; I believe it will always be that way. And we should stop fooling ourselves. Right? For instance, I cannot imagine some very, very capable novelist being invited to any international conference who does not exist as a writer simply because he writes his novels in Tswana. That's something; and we should stop fooling ourselves. And that the world does not know about him does not mean he does not exist as a very formidable force in the development of South African literature in the latter part of this century.

Poetry and society we are supposed to be talking about. I would like to say, at this time, without my little bitterness, frustration and anger, that I do not see the role of the writer—or, in this case, specifically the poet—as different from the role of anyone else in society or the role that the poet has ever played in any society in any century. If that poet has guts enough to be a poet, the preoccupations of any given epoch practically dictate what the preoccupation of the imaginative and creative mind is going to be. It is that simple. If you think of an urban, South African poet—urban, black, not urbanized, urban—who, when he says, "I come from Number 14 Getty Street, in Sophiatown," at least in my generation, there is no other place that he or she can point to as a home other than Number 14 Getty Street, in the way that, let us say, an Achebe or Ngugi can point away from Lagos and say *home*, or Ngugi point away from Nairobi and say *home*. That means even your sense of rhythm, for instance—even if you were describing rain clouds beginning to form—cannot be like the rural sense of rhythm that an Achebe would have. They would have the march or the rhythm of workers on strike, or at work; they might even have the rhythm of guerillas on an operation to destroy a plant. None of that mystical rural nonsense. Because this is 1987, and I think the quicker we deal with that, the better we'll be.

We are not struggling to get back to our ancestors' huts—mud huts are over with. South Africa is scientifically and technologically highly developed and we are an integral part and parcel of that. Western Native Township, where I grew up, was much, much more brutal, much more dangerous than the South Side of Chicago. And, should I lie to myself, about some little mud hut somewhere that I don't know anything about? No. And that brutality should inform my sensibility as a poet.

Thank you.

Anne McClintock: My first comment bears on a question raised by a number of previous speakers–the question of poetry's political legitimacy. At once the question of poetic value is raised, which is always itself a political question. Indeed one might say that South Africa has gone through three different phases with respect to the question of poetic legitimacy, and that these phases have their own political logic. After the destruction of Sophiatown in the fifties, most black poetry went underground, as writer after writer was gagged and stifled by bannings, detentions, suicides, murders and exile. Though black poets continued to write, very little of it was visible. White poets and critics continued to define poetic value within a very narrow colonial esthetic. In 1959 the Oxford University Press, for example, saw fit to publish *A Book of South African Verse* that featured thirty-two white male and four white female poets, yet included not a single black poet. Until the seventies, with a few exceptions, white publishing houses, journals and universities were effectively cordoned off from black experience by segregated education, severe censorship, bannings of writers and blocking of distribution, not to mention white condescension and indifference. But it seems that in the seventies white liberals–writers, poets, intellectuals, teachers and academics–began to sense that they were being edged out of cultural power by the nationalists. From their deepening sense of cultural loneliness, they began to court an alliance with black poets. There was a sense at this point of a need to selectively usher into the white poetic canon certain black writers who could be accommodated into the canon, and thereby bolster its dwindling legitimacy. At this point Oswald Mtshali's *Sounds of a Cowhide Drum* (Johannesburg: Renoster, 1971), was published. This marked the first phase of redefining poetic legitimacy: admitting into the canon certain texts which had hitherto been regarded as renegade or unfit.

But then South Africa witnessed an entirely new moment. With the Black Consciousness movement of the seventies, the question of black cultural values took center stage, as literacy campaigns, black theater and poetry readings were fostered in the belief that cultural nationalism was the road to political nationalism. Black poetry flourished at this time, as poetry workshops spread across the country, and as black poets, artists and writers insisted on the right to define poetic legitimacy in terms appropriate to the black communities. More importantly, however, after the Soweto rebellion, in the nervous climate of surveillance, bannings, censorship and loss of access to publication, poetry took flight from the established channels of publication and returned back into the black communities. As it turned out, poetry became a particularly agile medium for avoiding state attempts to curtail the explosion of black culture. Poetry was easier to memorize, and could be spread through the community much faster than, say, short stories or novels. Moreover, there was already a tenacious, indigenous tradition of oral poetry on which to draw. At this point an entirely new performative, communal poetry was forged, and performed before huge audiences at mass rallies, at USDF and trade-union meetings, in garages and cellars, often accompanied by music. So that poetry, in this entirely new communal and performative form, amounted to a vibrant integration of older traditional forms and more recent poetry. And this poetry played a vibrant role in keeping alive patterns of cultural resistance which were not possible in other established forms of print. At the same time, black poetry now presented a very real challenge to the "prestige of the literary," to established white assumptions about esthetic and poetic legitimacy, and to notions of poetry as transcendent, as somehow above the squalor of political polemics. Now the question of poetic legitimacy became inextricably entangled with questions about the politics of literacy, the politics of education and mass culture, the politics of cultural resistance, the role of the intellectuals and publishing houses, and so on.

All this bears on Kgositsile's comment that the South African poet is in no way unique. One can refer in this regard very briefly to another country where poetry has been seen to play a dynamic and urgent role in the social present and future of the country, namely Nicaragua. Ernesto Cardenal, the poet and Minister of Culture in Nicaragua, in a talk in 1981 at the closing of the national Celebration of Poetry Workshops, recalled how often he's asked why Nicaragua has so many and such good poets. In response, he pointed to the fact that something had happened in Nicaragua which had not happened elsewhere in the world, which was that peasants and workers, domestic workers and soldiers, were all writing poetry, and writing very good modern poetry. Now in answer to the question why, he answered that in Nicaragua the poets had always worked collaboratively, they had always worked in unity. An older poet like Ruben Darío had taken younger poets under his wing and had shared the poetic experience and had worked at teaching them. But the important point was that this wasn't an elite coterie of poets speaking to each other in an arcane and eloquent tongue, but rather working through workshops, which were beginning to spread through the country before the Sandinista revolution.

The reason I make this point is to emphasize that in fact a similar process has been taking place in South Africa. The significance of this for South Africans, and for the legitimacy of poetry, I feel, is that poetic expression has been appropriated by people in general, becoming a vital expression of social change, despite overwhelming odds. In the South African context, it seems very important that the formation of very popular, very widespread access to poetry, might create the potential for a post-revolutionary South African culture. The social legitimacy of poetry doesn't begin and end in bringing about social change; it has to continue after the revolution. And I think it's very important that the foundations of this more democratic culture be laid in South Africa. One question at this point is whether in recent years, with the emergence of worker theater and worker performance, the role of poetry is being superseded by theater, or whether we have a situation where they will work in alliance.

But this brings me to a second point, which arises from Ingrid de Kok's comments about the dilemmas facing women in writing. If, in Nicaragua, Cardenal identifies the strength of the poetic tradition as lying in collaborative unity, this at once raises a number of issues for women. The first is the bewildering absence of a female collaborative tradition. Miriam Tlali, looking back at the profusion of Sophiatown writing, asked, in some distress, "Where were the figures that my mother had spoken about? Where are my forebears, where are my ancestors? Who can I turn to as a model, as someone to learn from?" That's one particular dilemma: the historical erasure of women's writing. The second is the issue of the social legitimacy of women speaking in public. *Staffrider*, which as a number of you know is an important vehicle for popular poetry in South Africa, featured a number of issues in which women voiced their sense of uncertainty at challenging the male public domain. But by far the most urgent dilemma facing women is the social conditions of their work. Most women face the intolerable problem of the double day—returning from work as a domestic worker in a white family, say, only to work for her own husband and children, her own household, her own family, and the enormous burden that the double day places on her time and her energies makes it very difficult for a woman to go to rehearsals, or to poetry workshops, to take part in other kinds of community activities. This point is crucial for it is a problem that will remain with South African women even after revolutionary change.

Neville Choonoo: What struck me about the panel was the manner in which essentially there seems to be common ground that exists amongst us as South Africans that we are still struggling to find. I was thinking about the extent to which, in Afro-American literature anyway, it's interesting to see how Afro-American life and culture have informed American life to such a tremendous degree—informed its language and informed its manners, perhaps not as much politically—and yet in fact on college campuses around the nation black literature is still separated from courses in American literature. Thinking about that and thinking about the potential for creating a South African literature, I want to make a series of remarks which address themselves to the extent to which the diversity that exists in our country and which has been exploited by the state can in fact work to our advantage and be used by us to make the society a better one than it is.

My first observation, again about the *TriQuarterly* text, was how much several writers in South Africa are beginning to find common ground as the state becomes more and more totalitarian—as in fact groups like the UDF and the End Conscription Campaign, et cetera, find common ground in the face of the state, and how people like Jeremy Cronin, in fact, and to a certain extent Nadine Gordimer, are not only finding common ground in terms of their resistance to the state and their intolerance of the state, but also are becoming informed by the culture of black South Africa. To this extent I'd like to agree, then, with both Daniel Kunene, who this morning talked about the need for South Africans to begin not only to listen to but also to study the language and culture of fellow South Africans more intensely, and also with Mazisi's point that the old tradition in many ways needs to be looked at more carefully. But I want to add to that. I want to suggest that in fact South African literature right now seems to be still trying to find itself; I am quite struck by the extent to which all of us here as South Africans come from varied backgrounds, various linguistic backgrounds, and yet I'm always struck by the intensity of our sense of the country, and our love for it, which I think is common, and the extent to which this is manifested in the literature.

Ingrid de Kok brought up a point about the exploitation and the underrepresentation of white women in literature, and I cannot agree more. But perhaps I could suggest that that concern needs to be looked at within the broad concern of women in general in South Africa; there's been much talk about black women and their resistance and their being similarly left out, as it were, by the ANC [African National Congress]. I am wondering about the extent to which, in literature anyway, Ingrid would find models, especially in praise poetry, which could assist in finding an answer to that problem. I'm sorry that sounds so vague.

Keorapetse brought up some points which I'd like to respond to. I agree about his warning that we should stop gazing on ourselves, a sort of masturbating while the world watches us. I think his point is very important in terms of creating what I would call a common ground in our literary expression. I think that we are, all of us, born in South Africa, but I think we also are born into a place in South Africa—culturally, linguistically, and to a certain extent, or to a great extent, politically. And I think he's right in pointing out, if I understand him correctly, that that experience needs to be explored without any apology to anybody except to the extent that we, as writers—and this I feel very strongly about—need to be informed by the broad-based cultural energy which I think comes across very clearly in Alf's poetry. There seems to me, and I'm sure for you, a resonance, despite the fact that many do not understand the language; there seems to be a resonance and a deep tradition of which he speaks, which, regardless of our differences in the country, is something that strikes us right in the gut. And I want to say finally that I think a common literature is going to be created in South Africa when, in fact, we can identify ourselves within a South African tradition which is still struggling to be born. I'll leave it at that.

Thanks.

QUESTIONS AND ANSWERS:

Question: What opinion do the translators have about the necessity and difficulty of translation among the various languages spoken in South Africa?

Kgositsile: Translation is translation, whether it is from Japanese to English or French, or French to Russian, or whatever. It is difficult; there is nothing unique about the difficulty of translating from any South African language to any other South African language, or to Russian, Chinese, Mongolian or whatever. Again, I say we must stop petting ourselves; the sooner we stop these little masturbations in public; the sooner we can grapple with our reality the better. Sometimes I write in Tswana. I try to translate what I write into English, and I am not always too successful, and at times when I try to translate what I write in English into Tswana, I am not always particularly successful. That's all.

Bunn: I wanted to relate one of our experiences in putting together the magazine. We had tremendous difficulty with translation. One of the ways in which I found it useful to try to overcome the obstacles of translation, particularly from Afrikaans, was to work with the author. I think all translations, to be successful, have to be loose, have to be creative. To aim for some sort of reproduction in another language is fruitless, and in the attempt one often produces a text without life and vigor.

M. Kunene: I think it's almost impossible to accurately translate from one language to another and actually make a translation that has the full impact of the original text. I think it is necessary to make an interpretation of the text. That is why I agree with David, that you actually need the participation of the author in order for him to explain his own ideas and then interpret these ideas to make them accessible in translation. I do my own translation, but I'm not going to do any more. I think it's too much work! One takes more time translating the original text than in actually writing it. It's bad enough to be engaged day and night in writing–and then, to have to translate! I think there are some people who deserve to be given some grant, by some foundation, so that they can translate some African literature and make it accessible–whether in English, or in Afrikaans. I suppose if one had a more decent government, that's what you would want it to do. It would provide the means of communication across the linguistic barriers. One of the problems, I suppose, in translating the experience of Africans from African languages into European languages is that sometimes one is dealing with an entirely different perception of the world order. Sometimes a word may be similar, but the fundamental meaning may be quite different. So you have to interpret.

Ideas, also, are different. I think the translator must be steeped in the history of the people from whom he is translating, in the world-view, in an understanding of the society as a whole, and be able to interpret the strategies of their ideas, or the subtle nuances of their ideas. For instance, the African languages do a lot of suggestive approach–they don't usually explicitly state in detail what they want to project, they tend to make indirect comments and suggestions following a specific direction as defined by the word.

I think this activity is a normal activity, but it should be undertaken by the people who work with the author rather than hacks who want to make money.

D. P. Kunene: I have done some translating myself, and I talked a little bit about translation this morning. One word I used was that translation has to be "economical." I want to take issue with my colleague Kgositsile when he states that translating one African language into another is the same as translating an African language into, say, Japanese, and so on. I couldn't disagree more with that. When I talked about people not being economical in translation I meant, for example, that in translating a Zulu work into Xhosa, you are wastig resources, you're wasting time, you're wasting everything, because a Xhosa speaker can pick up a Zulu book and read it—with maybe a few problems here and there. If you translate a Tswana book into Sesotho, again, similarly, you're wasting time, because there is this great mutual interpenetrability between Tswana and Sesotho, and indeed among a whole group of languages in South Africa classified as the Sotho languages—that is the Sotho group, and again among a whole class of languages which are grouped as the Nguni group of languages, including Zulu, Xhosa, Swazi, et cetera, et cetera. And you can translate a poem, for example, much more effectively out of one of these languages into another—rhythms are much the same, grammatical structures are the same, and so on. There are tremendous resources within those languages that you can tap in order to maintain many of the original qualities.

So I must say that I was faced with a much more difficult situation translating Thomas Mofolo's chapter from Sesotho into English, or the two poems from Zulu that are published in *TriQuarterly*. So I think that you should not translate into languages that are so close that people can read them already. Languages from the Nguni group to the Sesotho group, yes: Zulu to Sesotho, Xhosa to Sesotho, et cetera, et cetera.

And then there was a question raised this morning that I want to mention very briefly here, about those tribal differences. The differences in many of them are more imaginary than real, and are created just in order to be used. We are very, very close in our languages, cultures and so on. And I think I'd like to say that translation essentially performs a very, very important task,

75

because we can't all speak all languages. We have to admit to our shortcomings in that respect.

[This session ended with a recitation of his poems by Alfred Temba Qabula.]

Culture and Politics in South Africa

Njabulo S. Ndebele
Ari Sitas, Hein Willemse,
Rob Nixon

"Struggle Continues" / linocut by Hamilton Budaza.

David Bunn: All conferences, I think, develop a character and a momentum of their own, and this one has acquired a particular personality, with all sorts of anecdotes and apocryphal stories going around. One of the nicest ones I've heard is the story of how Njabulo Ndebele is about to be bankrupted by his airport tax in Lesotho, accumulated by the many international trips he's made this year. Professor Ndebele is one of the most sought-after guest speakers in South Africa. He lectures in African, Afro-American and English literature at the University College of Roma, Lesotho. He holds an M.A. from Cambridge and a doctorate from the University of Denver. In 1984 he received a Noma Award for his magnificent collection of short stories, *Fools and Other Stories.* He's represented in *TriQuarterly* by the story "Death of a Son," and also by a major essay entitled "The English Language and Social Change in South Africa." Njabulo Ndebele is fast emerging as one of the most influential critics of South African literature and cultural and intellectual production. He's also the president of the newly-formed Congress of South African Writers. I can think of nobody better suited to lead our session on South African culture, the session in which we will try to at least begin theorizing the future.

Njabulo S. Ndebele: Thank you, David.

This talk that I'm going to be giving today is entitled "Towards Progressive Cultural Planning." This is an aspect of my thoughts about the state of culture in South Africa today, and I have to say that because of the momentum of events, this particular paper is a revised version of one that I delivered about two or three months ago in Durban, where another significant cultural event was taking place. The students of the University of Durban, Westville, were attempting to found a new alternative tradition, to make a contribution to it in the form of a cultural festival that will challenge the currently popular existing one that takes place from Grahamstown in the Cape. It is hoped that this one–this cultural festival, which will be an annual event–will be an alternative to the traditional one, which, in the view of many people who are serious thinkers on the South African situation, is strongly and firmly anchored in the status quo.

A South African scholar by the name of Peter Horn, a professor of German at the University of Cape Town, begins an essay of his with an observation which is pertinent to the subject of this paper. He says:

> It is not true to say that there is no culture of
> the oppressed: but it is true to say that, where
> the oppressed are forcibly separated from their
> own political and cultural organizations, the
> influence of the media on the consciousness of
> the oppressed is much greater than in those
> countries where they create and distribute their
> own information through their own media.[1]

I'm not sure what research Peter Horn conducted to arrive at this particular conclusion. But I would put in

---

1. Peter Horn, "A Preparatory Note on Peter Weiss, His Novel, *The Aesthetics of Resistance* and Its Relevance to the South African Situation," *Critical Arts*, Vol. 3, No. 4, p. 1.

the word 'tend' to influence the consciousness of the oppressed," because I think the oppressed themselves are responding to that pressure in various ways.

But this observation, nevertheless, reminds me of an analogous situation, at the level of a particular individual experience, in which Ariel Dorfman describes the transformation and awakening of a poor woman from one of the slums of Chile. While this woman, very much under the influence of the kind of media Peter Horn alludes to, had previously insisted on her reading diet of escapist "industrial products of fiction,"[2] something was to happen to her during the time of Salvador Allende's brief presidency which changed her attitude completely. Dorfman makes a general observation to the effect that:

> When a people attempts to liquidate centuries' worth of economic and social injustice, when they begin to gain a sense of their dignity as a nation, what is really at stake, what really inspires them, is an alternate vision of humanity, a different way of feeling and thinking and projecting and loving and keeping faith. And a different future.[3]

He then comments on the specific case of the woman from the slums:

> That woman from the slums was being shoved, poked, awakened. And while she was in that turbulent, searching stage, what she needed was a parallel interpretation at all levels [I want to emphasize at all levels] of what her situation, of what the world, was. Not just a political explanation of why things were one way and how they might be trans-

2. Ariel Dorfman, *The Empire's Old Clothes* (New York: Pantheon, 1983), p. 3.
3. Ibid., p. 5.

formed, but channels for expressing the joys, the doubts, the anxieties that come when people who were previously powerless begin to have some say in their existence. What she needed was a new language.[4]

How is this relevant to our discussion of culture and politics in South Africa today, since this was the general topic of this afternoon? If we define culture broadly as Horn and Dorfman simply, clearly seem to do, then we shall appreciate the extent of the South African problem in terms of the perspective from which I'm going to attempt to look at it.

A useful point of departure is Marek, Hromadka and Chroust's description of culture in their UNESCO document on cultural policy in Czechoslovakia. They write that:

> Culture as a social process is an entire, internally structured system, in which we usually distinguish two aspects: material culture (sometimes denoted by the term "civilization") and spiritual culture. The term "material culture" is usually applied to the material results of human work, as for instance to machines, technology, buildings, settlements, the mode of sustenance and clothing, the objects of everyday use. The term "spiritual culture" is usually applied to an aspect of the cultural process which is oriented to the human soul, which creates and forms a man's intellect, ideas, feelings, ethical and aesthetic standards, attitudes and behaviour; cultural values influence among others man's psychology and mode of living, and represent in principle the material results of human findings

---

4. Ibid., p. 5.

and knowledge in science, art and in the sphere of social standards.[5]

Now, the racist system of South Africa has systematically denied the oppressed majority a meaningful opportunity for creative involvement in the entire arena of cultural practice. It is not only that obstacles have been placed in their way in the fields of writing, painting and music and the other arts, for example, through censorship, but also that specifically they have not had any say whatsoever in socially organized planning of society as a whole. They have had no say in the planning of their communities; in the designing and the building of the houses they live in; in the making of the clothes they wear; in the making of decisions regarding the safety of food, cosmetics and medicines; in the determination of research priorities in science and technology; in discussions regarding the devaluation of the national currency; in the establishment of banks; in the formulation of agricultural policy; in the establishment of prisons, mental asylums and hospitals; in decisions regarding the transportation of goods and people; in decisions to demolish old historical buildings or to build museums.

Characterized in these specific ways, political deprivation is given, it seems to me, a concrete social, cultural form. What this suggests is that the oppressed were effectively denied the opportunity and sovereign right and experience to create a complex human civilization consciously. This picture should serve to indicate the enormous task of reconstruction ahead, which will be undertaken in the attempt to enable the oppressed in South Africa to discover a new, rich and very complex social language of their own.

---

5. Miroslav Marek, Milan Hromadka and Josef Chroust, *Cultural Policy in Czechoslovakia* (Paris: UNESCO, 1970), p. 15.

One major consequence of this situation is that, over the decades, the condition of sustained and brutal oppression appears to have placed the burden of organized, organic cultural expression on political resistance. But because of the relatively weak capability of the oppressed, at the time, to deploy vast material resources to challenge their oppression, much of their means of resistance was dominated by the rhetorical articulation of political grievance. This means that the armory of resistance became largely abstract, not in a pejorative sense of the word, but in the sense that the struggle became more and more a matter of articulating injustice and declaring goals, although there was a lot of action, in the process, meant to give it a material dimension, which was by and large not successful.

All the more, then, could the system deploy an array of ideological weapons—the media, for example—to influence the perceptions of the oppressed, since about three-quarters of the terrain of battle was effectively uncontested. The oppressed did not have an army of industrialists, of engineers, of architects or scientists, and a host of other professionals with which to contest domination with the entire range of material culture, and thus, with a practical sense of the interconnectedness, the organic unity, of organized social activity.

Within this terrain of ideological conflict, two major approaches to the question of cultural resistance have dominated discussion. The first one I will call the restorative approach, in which attempts were made, and are still being made with remarkable success to reveal and to restore to the oppressed the history of their cultural practices. Because the culture of the oppressed as a whole was and continues to be the target of imperialism. One of the major ways by which imperialistic intervention was justified was to deny the existence of this indigenous culture. Consequently, for example, when literature, virtually at gunpoint at the time of conquest, as well as under the influence of the emergent marketplace of capitalism, and the implications for social organization and control which this new system entailed, when literature became synonymous in our case with English literature, and civilization became synonymous with western culture, then the culture of the oppressed, as they had lived it before their domination, effectively ceased to exist. Amílcar Cabral puts it this way:

> History teaches us that, in certain circumstances, it is very easy for the foreigner to impose his domination on a people. But it likewise teaches us that, whatever the material aspects of this domination, it can be maintained only by the permanent and organized repression of the cultural life of the people concerned. Implantation of domination can be ensured definitively only by physical elimination of a significant part of the dominated population.
>
> In fact, to take up arms to dominate a people is, above all, to take up arms to destroy, or at least to neutralize and to paralyze their cultural life. For as long as part of that people can have a cultural life, foreign domination cannot be sure of its perpetuation. At a given moment, depending on internal and external factors determining the evolution of the society in question, cultural resistance (indestructible) may take on new...forms, in order fully to contest foreign domination.[6]

In response to this kind of onslaught, the call for restoration was also made by Kwame Nkrumah, among others, back in the early sixties when he declared:

> In the New African renaissance, we place great emphasis on the presentation of history. Our

---

6. Amilcar Cabral, *Unity and Struggle* (London: Heinemann [AWS], 1980), pp. 139-40.

history needs to be written as the history of
our society, not as the story of European ad-
ventures.[7]

But such a call was not new. Similar calls predate
Nkrumah's call by several decades. Writers such as Tiyo
Soga, Sol Plaatje, [Zakea] Mangoaela and others, quite
early in the modern struggle against imperialism, were
already producing committed literature, partly with the
intention of preventing the total loss and destruction of
African culture. But then a conspiracy of silence, as a result of the culture of racism and imperialism, prevented
the publication and distribution of such works. They
virtually ceased to exist. Consequently, the work of such
writers had to be resuscitated, and that is why in recent
times, heeding the call of decolonization, many African
historians have shed much revealing and liberating light
on the history of our continent. Similarly, literary historians have brought to the surface a rich body of African literature which, only yesterday, was never even
thought to exist. This kind of resuscitating work should
and will no doubt continue well into the future, as all
oppressed communities in South Africa have suffered
from the concerted silencing of their cultures.
    It can be said, then, that the work of restoration
was designed to put before the minds of the oppressed
the historical image of a legitimate and well-organized
social life—that is to say, an image of civilization built by
their ancestors. This was done in order to suggest that
the organized social strivings of the past could be repeated.
    The other approach to this question of cultural re-
sistance has concerned itself with analyzing cultural
practice, particularly with regard to the arts in terms of
either their emotional or their intellectual effect on society. Here the emphasis is on the capacity of cultural
activity to influence social behavior in the fulfillment of

_____
7. Kwame Nkrumah, *Consciencism: Philosophy and Ideology
for De-Colonisation* (London: Panaf, 1964), p. 63.

specific social objectives. Taking the particular example of literature, we immediately become aware of the extensive terrain covered by this approach in terms of the relationship between literature and society. How should writers reflect society? Should they write novels, short stories or poems? What should they write about? Who should they write about? Who are the readers of their books? What are the class origins of writers, and what are their positions on political issues? What is the relationship between a writer's political convictions and his work? Where should writers publish their work, and how best can their work be distributed? How do we train more writers? What are the levels of literacy in society? Exactly how do literary works impact on social behavior? The questions are many and often difficult to answer. But they are constantly being grappled with by writers themselves, by professional critics, as well as by all kinds of people interested in literature. Much of the discussion of literature will almost invariably center around any one of the questions posed.

Today I would like to pose yet another question. In the reconstruction of society, what progressive societal role do we ascribe to cultural practice in the South African context? How do we free ourselves from notions of culture that are tied to the ethos of oppression? When we probe a little further into this question we will note that it is not only cultural action itself that is under scrutiny, but also the kind of institutional arrangement created for the practice and promotion of cultural activity. Specifically, what would be the progressive attitude towards theater halls, opera houses, cinemas, sports fields, concert halls, libraries, art galleries, museums, schools, universities, research institutes, the civil service, the institutions of commerce and industry, and a host of other facilities created for the purpose of promoting broad cultural activity?

However, since the field is so vast, I shall limit my discussion to the narrow field of the arts, in the interests of both brevity and clarity.

Of course, I cannot pretend to have answers to these questions, because the problems are complex. Perhaps the current phase of the struggle has to assume a much firmer organizational form in terms of the necessary institutionalization of progressive ideas. For example, to what extent does the answer lie in the successful consolidation of the concepts of street committees, of people's courts, people's education, and other emergent alternative grass-roots forms of social organization? Clearly then, the question one is asking is in essence a political one, and one which is fraught with implications for social action, since political objectives ultimately derive their legitimacy and efficacy from the success of practical creative social action. It does mean, then, that the clarity of political objectives is fundamental.

The starting point for all of us—at the moment, basing myself on my experience, on my reading of the mass-based democratic movement that is taking place in South Africa at the moment—the starting point is the uncompromising demand for democracy. This democracy will necessarily assume forms that take into account the history of our oppression. One visible factor of this history has been our enforced silence. This enforced silence also affected communication among ourselves, thus blunting our intellectual growth. Hence our hunger for knowledge, our hunger for speech, our hunger for constructive social discussion, our hunger for the ultimate right—the right to determine the future with our minds as well as with our hands. Much of our energy will be turned in that direction. One way through which our voice can be heard is the way of art, and since we seek a consonance between all creative social activity on the one hand, and the collective political will on the other, we have to state that the social relevance of art will have to be defined in the context of that search.

Confronted with concerted pressure from the oppressed, the South African government at the moment is seeking to find ways of accommodating the aspirations of the oppressed without having to give up effective power. The technique is to persuade the oppressed that the existing structures of social and political organization are open to them on condition that the ways in which they function are not altered. So it is with all the other benefits of science and technology. In other words, the seemingly objective efficacy of science and technology is a matter beyond debate.

The resulting policy of reform that is so popular today in sectors of the South African government is based on the premise of the objective validity of the oppressors' own cultural practice and the results thereof. This reasoning, of course, is fundamentally flawed.

I would like to attempt a preliminary analysis of this problem by quoting at length the work of an American radical psychiatrist, Joel Kovel, who provides us with a very useful analogy in a book called *The Age of Desire,* and the relevant chapter, "The Administration of the Mind":

> Consider a simple and seemingly neutral example: consider the necessity for traffic lights in the big city, "rationally" timed to ensure the flow of traffic. Traffic "naturally" tends to be chaotic, since the human organism cannot regulate the great power of the automobile. Enter a bureau of traffic and a traffic engineer who impersonally studies the flow of traffic, figures out the problem mathematically, and sets up a system of lights. And behind him enters the traffic police to impersonally enforce the law which, by saying one has to stop for lights, caps off the whole process of traffic rationalization. Now everyone is happy, for no one can force his way across intersections without paying a penalty. Even the tycoon, who can buy his way out of anything, pauses before the impersonal majesty of the traffic law, partly to forestall nuisance, partly out of concern for the dangers

inherent in violating the law. People readily internalize the discipline of traffic signals. The most unruly lout will, in the vast majority of instances, stop at the red and go at the green. Even psychotics readily obey.

But when we focus on the rational need for bureaucratic intervention into the social complexity of traffic, we can lose sight of the reality behind the complexity. The flow of traffic in a city is primarily determined by the needs to get workers to and from the workplace and consumers to and from the stores; and secondarily, but equally deeply, determined by the need to keep markets expanding for corporate behemoths who fatten on traffic: oil companies, automobile manufacturers, road builders, et cetera. Therefore, the complexity of traffic is a direct function of the exigencies of capital accumulation. And capital accumulation can never relent; its very success only feeds its chaotic tendencies. The more "efficient" the traffic lights make the system at one level, the more uncontrolled they will make it, and the society it defines, at another level, the level of pollution, of energy squandering, inflation, technological unemployment, mechanization of work, imbecility of culture, and so forth.[8]

What this analysis reveals, among other things, is that we should learn to resist the manner in which the capitalist marketplace attempts to lull us into a sense of false complacency by giving us the impression that it is objectively efficient. It will build universities, concert halls, art galleries, sports fields, and a host of other social amenities, but for what purpose? For sure, a

8. Joel Kovel, *The Age of Desire* (New York: Pantheon, 1981), pp. 170-71.

soccer stadium is a good thing, but is it unimportant that today in South Africa we associate soccer teams with products advertised on their jerseys as well as all over the stadium rather than with the efficacy of physical culture? Sport has become money. Our traffic lights, therefore—no doubt a result of valuable science and technology—are a convenience which may also serve extremely complex ideological ends.

But before we go further into this matter, let us look at the kind of conspiracy that can exist between the corporate world and the seemingly elevating world of culture. We look at an example that comes from our own history.

Tim Couzens, in a significant piece of restorative work, reveals how way back in the 1920's and 1930's, film was used as a means of controlling labor in the mines. The book is called *The New African: A Study of the Life and Work of H.I.E. Dhlomo,* and the relevant chapter is entitled "Moralizing Leisure Time" (1918-1936). In this chapter, Couzens seeks to show how "culture and entertainment can be used as an auxiliary force in social control."[9] A group of white, liberal missionaries in the 1920's, faced with the large influx of Africans into the cities, the rise of slums and their attendant social problems, as well as the recent Land Act of 1914, sought to find ways of rescuing Africans from such a potentially corrupting social environment, while also stemming the tide of the potential political discontent that may rise to uncontrollable heights among Africans. They had two targets: "the blacks who lived and worked in the city and mine laborers in the compounds."[10] Attempts were to be made to educate these blacks through entertainment.

In the mines, film was going to be used for this purpose: "We must capture the physical and mental life

9. Tim Couzens, *The New African: A Study of the Life and Work of H.I.E. Dhlomo* (Johannesburg: Ravan, 1985), p. 92.
10. Ibid., p. 93.

of these young men during six days of the week besides preaching the Gospel to them on the seventh," wrote Reverend Ray Philips.[11] After volleyball and soccer had somewhat caught on, the magic of film did the job. Here is how Reverend Philips described the success of film:

> The result was immediate and gratifying. The thousands gathered around the screen and showed their appreciation by filling the compounds so full of joyful sound that outsiders often decided that a riot was occurring. With amazed delight the happy crowds went off on trips on the modern magic carpet to other lands; saw the surf riders of Honolulu, the explorers in the Arctic, the reindeer of Lapland and the potter's wheel in India. They followed with quaking breath the adventures of some of the early pioneers among the Indians in Western America; saw King George go to open Parliament in his curious equipage. But they shook their heads at pictures of mining in England and America, showing white men at work with pick and shovel and drill: "Aikona! No, that is not right! Mfundisi is fooling us here! No white man works like that. Only black men!"[12]

Now, no doubt a picture of childlike, enthralled miners was proof of how easy it would be to keep them busy. It is possible that if further study were made on this subject it might reveal that the apparent success of the program of filmed shows in the mines led to a general government policy on the provision of entertainment to the rest of the African population throughout the country.

---

11. Ibid., p. 96.
12. Ibid., p. 96.

However, for the urban African, more sophisticated plans were afoot. Social centers were to be provided where the urban dweller would participate in such activities as reading, debates, indoor games, the production of plays, and ballroom dancing. Boy Scout and Girl Guide movements would take care of the young. Thus concludes Couzens on the salutary effects of reading, according to R.H.W. Shepherd, one of the "culturalists":

> While there is no evidence for insincerity or hypocrisy on Shepherd's part, a distinct pattern of underlying assumptions emerges from his actions and writings. Clearly the activity of reading and the institution of libraries were important ways in which blacks could be acculturated into the "new civilization" whose value was scarcely doubted. The values of "good literature" would thus be inculcated and the calm, dispassionate sedentary nature of the activity would no doubt be salutary.[13]

What is of particular interest to us about these examples from the past is not so much the films themselves, or the other cultural activities as such, for their value or lack of value would be the proper subject of another discussion. What should be of real interest to us is the actual provision of physical facilities: film-showing arenas, mobile libraries, gramophones and records, social centers such as the Bantu Men's Social Center, the YMCA and the YWCA. Later we would have what came to be called Community Halls and Community Schools. Particular facilities were provided for the specific purpose of using cultural practice for social control. Underlying these institutions, therefore, is a particular notion of art: art civilizes natives by exposing them to western culture and thus reducing their capacity to resist that culture in its totality. And that total-

---

13. Ibid., pp. 105-06.

ity includes its political and economic institutions and the laws governing their operation. Culture was designed to socialize the oppressed into accepting the foreign parameters of their domination. These facilities, therefore, were created for the purposes of acculturation.

It should not be difficult to appreciate why for the majority of the urban oppressed, particularly the petty bourgeoisie, it was the form of the medium of culture rather than the message that was the focus of interest, for the form was easily associated with advancement. Reading maketh a man. But what do you read? What is is the context in which the reading takes place? And so, I suppose, does ballroom dancing also maketh a man. And so does going to the movies. It does not matter that you're going to see the Lone Ranger, Tarzan and Donald Duck cartoons. The point is, being there, where a film is being shown, is advancement. Consequently, there developed an imitative cultural behavior generally lacking in content. It is this that became the "official" culture of the townships.

All these "cultural" activities would take place in what came to be called Community Halls or Community Schools or buildings such as the Bantu Men's Social Center, built for that purpose. The names of these buildings, you can see, identify their designated ideological function. They indicate their origins in colonial anthropology to designate facilities for "culturally backward" people. In this context, then, these facilities performed the function of acculturation and were not meant to provide occasions in which people would be able to reflect seriously on themselves and their environment. This situation has continued up until today.

Central to the quest for liberation in South Africa today is the quest for knowledge: the kind of knowledge that would lead to, and be, a significant contribution to the struggle for liberation. It is this knowledge that will enable the oppressed to speak with a new voice. Clearly, if what the oppressed masses of South Africa want to get back is their voice, if, as a result, everything at the moment is content—for there is no doubt that the art of the moment is that form that offers most the promise of the advancement of knowledge and the deepening of insight (I'm thinking here of all forms of art involving the word, whether articulated or writ-ten)—then, as far as art is concerned, we have to refocus our understanding of its place in society. The example of literature may be helpful here.

Where, before, reading was a mere function of social advancement; where it had been chiefly an indicator of acculturation; where it had been a functional activity to enable workers to read instructions and become better servants; where to read fiction has been to read industrially produced romance and superstition; now, the more creative, liberating and positive values of reading have to be restored. Reading has to be seen as the deepening of insight; as the broadening of intellectual horizons in the serious search for solutions to problems thrown up, in the first instance, by our immediate environment; as a vehicle of vital information about that environment; and—no less importantly—as the enjoyment of, as well as a reflection on, the miracle of human language.

Politically, reading will be seen and regarded as an important extension of the democratic process itself. For reading is one of those social activities in the context of which ideas ought necessarily to be debated, and one which also contributes to the development of a critical social habit of thought. The need, then, in general, is that we entertain the notion, in our struggle, of "committed leisure," in which our attitude towards what are known presently as places of entertainment becomes a lot more serious. Theaters, according to this view, become places to which we go not because we want to show how cultured we are, but because we are going to explore with the actors issues that concern us deeply. Theater, then, becomes a place in which the issues addressed in lecture rooms (such as this one), in centers

95

of government, are explored within the leisurely, though no less serious, context of drama. It is in this sense that I say that art should, properly speaking, be regarded as an extension of the democratic process. Only from that perspective can we really appreciate the fundamental social need for it.

The implications for this on the character of progressive political intervention in culture should already be evident. The political wing of the struggle—no doubt in the forefront of this struggle—should not make concessions to cultural practice. They should plan for it as a matter of necessity, for it is the only social context in which people are uninhibitedly themselves. For this reason, we should not "include" culture as an afterthought in social planning. On the contrary, we should say, there can be no democratic society without the progressive institutionalization of cultural practice, in all its forms.

The matter can be restated differently. The arts should not be regarded as a mere means to an end—as a means to manipulate public thought, for example. That is one function they can play. But that function can degenerate into being a purely manipulative venture in which even those in the forefront of the struggle can use art to limit and contain the expressive capacity of the people. For that reason, the manipulative function of art can be a potentially reactionary one. The need is consciously to accord the arts a structural function in society. The justification for this need should derive from the nature of the society we envisage rather than from a limited political program. The function of art in society should outlive the limits of a specific political program of action. In other words, instead of asserting that we need the arts to mobilize people, as a primary goal, rather we should say we need the arts because they extend limits of democratic participation. So it should be with cultural practice in general.

At issue is a rigorous critique of existing cultural practice and institutions and a determined groping towards fundamental and liberating alternatives. We aim not only at changing the content of our cultural expression, but also at efficient social organization where such expression can be assigned a definite place. The aim is to restore to the community of the oppressed a practical sense of organized and organic civic society. This, I believe, could be done through a concerted focus on the actual material dimensions of civic society. For the oppressed do have a culture; what they need to do is pay closer attention to its material expression during the process of struggle, so that that culture itself can constitute the real content of a changing alternative consciousness.

We are going to be heirs to a highly complex industrial and technological culture which may even include a nuclear arsenal. What an awesome responsibility! The aim is not to allow ourselves to be overwhelmed by this culture and the rigidly entrenched methods of its operation, which have become second nature to those whose behavior has been completely conditioned by it. Rather, it is to understand it, throwing away all its evils while making its best aspects available to the enrichment of the emergent and highly creative alternative culture. That would be the nature of our contribution to the universal struggle for liberty.

I thank you.

Reginald Gibbons: There will be responses from three other participants who will speak in the order you see them, from right to left, Ari Sitas, followed by Hein Willemse, followed by Rob Nixon.

Ari Sitas: Thank you. Njabulo Ndebele has posed some questions that have no easy answers. For example, how do we free ourselves from notions of culture that are tied to the ethos of oppression? How do we go beyond the institutions of cultural activity? What progressive role can we imagine culture to play in the broader movement for democracy? Now, I would like to respond in an oblique way by etching—or better, by molding—my argument out of the lives and times of cultural activists in Natal's labor movement, a molding process which Alfred Temba Qabula started this morning. And here I shall use my experiences, as it were, of this experience, to attempt to answer some of these questions.

Over the last five years, Natal has been the cradle of a robust cultural movement, alongside trade-union organization. Everywhere up and down the country, as Qabula said today, *izimbongi* (oral poets) are spewing out their "words of fire," dancers are shining leather and cutting shoes, performers are acting out grotesque and realistic pieces of drama, and everywhere there is an explosion of cultural energy. Now, on the one hand, this is spontaneous. On the other, there is argument and structure. To quote from some of the documents of this cultural activity, "We have been singing, parading, boxing and acting and writing within the system we did not control. So far black workers have been feeding all their creativity into a cultural machine to make profits for others. We must begin to control our creativity. We must create a space in our struggle through our own songs, our own slogans, our own poems, our own activities, our own plays and dances. We must conquer, yes, but our struggle is not there only to destroy institutions of oppression; it is there to build new ones, embodying our principles of democracy of, of unity and of our new

98

world." The cultural activists of Natal's black working class have begun to create alternative institutions for their self-expression.

South Africa's labor movement, for instance, was praised this morning by Alfred Qabula as a swaying, moving black forest of Africa. The cultural activists—to extend the metaphor—can be seen as that forest's gwala-gwala birds (purple-crested loerie or knyona loerie birds), those beautiful, stark, primary-colored birds that fly from branch to branch inside the forests. In other words, their struggle is to make the swaying forest synonymous or simultaneous with the existence of these forms of beauty. I'll come back to the metaphor at the end.

Now, let's discuss the forest. Most of you know that in the early 1970's, attempts were made to organize black workers into trade unions. Initially, there was a trickle of workers, who were pockmarked with worry, going to dingy little offices, pouring out their issues—and, without any warning, there was a flood. In 1973 the general strikes in Durban created the impetus for modern, as it were, post-1970's trade unionism. And this trade unionism was unique in two ways: firstly, it relied on a grass-roots form of democracy and accountability; secondly, by the 1980's it became a trade unionism dissimilar and different from any other kind of trade unionism advanced capitalist countries have known. It was, to find a better word, like a poor people's movement, or like a social movement, of a peculiar kind. Still, in these larger and larger gatherings that started developing, what was dormant, what was latent or undefeated or uncontrolled, started exploding with carnival-like intensity. And from the smaller meetings to the bigger ones you started having the proliferation of cultural activities.

At the same time there was a realization that old lives became unlivable, but new ones were not possible. And a lot of this experience was caught in this limbo: you can't go back to the old way of life, and yet the new one you desire is not yet possible. And with this desire there were other ingredients that made the chemistry of this process, where everything—oral forms, dances, poetry, writing, all these items—were thrown into the melting pot to create a robust cultural contribution. And it was interesting, in another way, that some of the crucial initial cultural activists now became important labor leaders in Natal, and they swept cultural activity with them. They wanted their own cultural activists there in the forefront with them. So, throughout all that, a new tension developed, and this tension—which is a very delicate balancing act—has the following form: trade unions want cultural activity because it is a diversion in meetings, on the one hand, or because it functions as a union propaganda machine, on the other. At the same time, on the other side of this balancing act, you get these cultural activists—who all of a sudden found a space in which to express themselves—wanting to engage in cultural activity in its own right. And that tension, at the moment, is a creative one.

To go back to our gwala-gwala bird, it's interesting that the name of the bird derives from its shrieks of horror at the approach of creatures that are to devour it. It is interesting, also, that that bird is hunted for its feathers, to be used for ceremonies of chiefs in the old days, of homeland institutions these days. And now that shriek is developing in intensity as waves and waves of violence are descending on these cultural activists who are struggling to break through.

So, to go back to the questions that were raised: how do we free ourselves from notions of culture that are tied to the ethos of oppression? A simple answer would be by allowing all this flourishing activity, not only in the labor movement, to proliferate; and, in these forms of self-organization of ordinary people, to insist that the ethos is democratic.

Next question: how do we go beyond the institutions of cultural activity? The lesson here seems to be: create new ones that allow for maximum popular participation.

The third question: what progressive role can we imagine culture to play in the broader movement for democracy? I think we can imagine culture to play a fundamental role in the construction of a democratic society, because through this kind of democracy, both in form and content, we can create the vision for a better future for all of us in South Africa.

Hein Willemse: I'm going to be much briefer than Ari, and perhaps, just before I begin, I think I should comment on the significance of Njabulo's paper, because I think the paper in itself is extremely significant in its historical timing. The mere fact that Njabulo has chosen this particular topic at this particular historical time, I think reveals something of his reading of the political situation as well. That in itself to me seems very important, very significant. The mere fact that at this stage we can actually start talking about planning, about what's going to happen in the future, about the way we see things, the way we would like things to develop—that in itself I think is important. You probably recall, those of you steeped in the debate on African literatures, South African literature, you probably recall that in previous sessions of this nature, people would speak about "protest literature," would speak about "resistance literature," "resistance in culture." The mere fact that we can at this stage talk about cultural planning, planning ahead, in itself can be significant. So, given that approach, I think one needs to analyze the complex nature of South African society and realize that not only is there that confidence that we have in the South African environment [the South African oppressed]—despite three States of Emergency, despite the current state of affairs in the country, the more repressive nature of the South African state—the fact that we start talking about cultural planning and we actually do that with renewed vigor is in itself an indication of the material advantages that we have made in the struggle over the last couple of years.

And there are four points I would like to comment on. One is cultural hegemony. I think what the paper has mentioned a couple of times was the place of culture alongside the political movement—and now, by Ari, in the labor movement. What for me is important is that we should stop talking about the way in which culture or cultural forms can become part of the oppressed's hegemony in South Africa. Let me explain that in terms of the power of the sign, the power of discourse—the fact that in some cases the oppressed's notion of themselves has become the notion, has become the definition. This morning somebody mentioned the so-called "colored" and so-called "whites" and so-called "Indians" and so on. Just take that example—the notion of separate entities, tribes and so on, has been created by the ruler, and the mere fact that people at this stage, over the last couple of years, have taken the power to name themselves, that in itself is extremely important. It's a cultural act to name yourself, to call yourself by a particular name.

So when, for instance, people said—in the period of black consciousness—we are not coloreds and Indians and Bantus, we group ourselves under "black people," that in itself was a very important step to take. For at that stage, black people then took the power of naming themselves, took control of the discourse. So in that sense the cultural act itself is streets ahead of the political action. Now the ruler had to go back, had to retreat, in a sense. In Afrikaans, for instance, it's not common nowadays—in government pronouncements—to talk about "coloreds." They will talk about "the brown people" or they will talk about "people of color," but underlying that is the fact that black people gained control over the discourse, over the limits and the definitions of naming themselves.

And that in itself is very powerful. Just take that example—the sort of cultural hegemony that is developing when people start talking about "the limits of cultural expression," the ways of culturally expressing themselves. Over the years, in the labor movement and political meetings and otherwise, the hegemony that has been created in the cultural arena and cultural terrain is something that I think we need to build on, that needs to be institutionalized. Not perhaps in the sense that we have to create physical institutions for it, like a festival or something like that. It would help, it would go along—but just in that little manner of discourse, already there is an extremely important means of gaining control.

And my last point, on the changing forms in cultural expression. Somebody this morning said—and I would link this with Njabulo's paper—I think the person spoke about "the older forms," and said they were nonsense. Let's look exactly at what we need to do. I think some of those older cultural forms we cannot just destroy, because we have to inform them with new meaning. For instance, take the aspect of the *imbongi* in oral poetry. Why is it that in South Africa there is a very strong tradition of the *imbongi*? I would think that the new place of the *imbongi* is in the trade-union movement—there's a changed position from the old position and from the relationship to a particular group of people, the particular societal relationship. That relationship between the *imbongi* and his audience changed completely, to such an extent that the cultural norm now, or the political importance of the cultural act, is something of great significance within the economy, with the political utterances of people. That extends to the level in which we see democracy.

That extends to the way in which we see democracy developing in South Africa. Again, I don't think that you can talk about democracy as if it's a neutral term, as if it's something that is just out there. Njabulo hasn't mentioned this, and I would take the liberty of informing you about the particular politics underlying the notion of democracy in South Africa—that is developing through struggle and through culture as well. And the questions of mandate, the questions of consultation—for instance, the fact that you have to consult with a particular organization; the fact that you need to respond to a collective—that in itself is part of the developing cultural terrain and the cultural hegemony that I think we are gaining.

Thank you.

Rob Nixon: I'm going to pick up on some of these questions of institutional arrangements, mass media, cultural accommodation, very briefly, and from a somewhat different perspective, partly because I'm someone who grew up in the country but has spent several years in the United States now. And I feel, as there are so many people speaking from the ground up, who have flown in recently, that perhaps one of the more instructive things I can do is to talk a little bit from the interface—looking at how I perceive the South African cultures of resistance being packaged and transmitted in the context of the United States.

My initial assumption would be that when any kind of cultural activity or product travels from one society to another, it's going to be refracted. You can't expect perfect transmission. The needs and concerns of the society that it arrives in are going to be different, and it is going to be in some senses a compromise between the issues at home and the history, the concerns, the ambitions, of the society it arrives in. I'll take a couple of literary examples and maybe one or two political ones.

For a long time Athol Fugard's theater had hegemony, really, in America and in Britain. And one of the successful endeavors to break up that hegemony and complicate the view of South African theater was the Woza Afrika Festival that was held in New York and Washington last year. It was interesting comparing productions of those plays in South Africa, in Harlem and at the Lincoln Center. One of the things that interests me here is that particularly as so much of the current cultural resistance—the future-oriented culture of South Africa—is, as people have been saying all day, very much performance-oriented, it seems as if context (the social context, the audience of those performances) plays a much stronger role in how those are received and read. So translation isn't simply a linguistic problem, it's a problem of context.

And what struck me was that the theater of resistance in South Africa, coming to the United States, intersects with a very different theatrical tradition. Here theater is, in a sense, struggling to survive a rearguard battle against the hegemony of the moving image, whether it's TV or film. In the South African situation the battle is against physical violence, state intimidation, prohibitions on public gatherings. Somehow, some kind of middle ground is struck in this context. The distance between these traditions, and, if you like, the imperfection of the transmission, was reflected in some of the criticisms that theater reviewers meted out to these plays. It wasn't always clear to me whether some of the esthetic judgments that were made did not come out of an almost frustrated metropolitan alienation from even being able to imagine the kind of audience and the kind of political importance that those cultural happenings could have in South Africa.

One of the quotes I thought was particularly telling was from the *Village Voice* critic. He started off describing the plays as agitprop and then said, "But we have to acknowledge that they're dangerous enough in the South African situation for serious intimidation to take place." So you've got the dilemma of material that the metropolitan critic doesn't want to recognize as art, but that is dangerously effective. And in a sense, you could feel through his reading that it was an inversion of the circumstances of New York theater—which is, in his terms, esthetically valuable but scarcely socially dangerous. And his comment was that "It's frustrating and infuriating that these plays are more threatening to the hideous Botha than flies to wanton boys." In other words, that in a sense it was completely incomprehensible that these could be politically powerful yet from within the tradition of American theater they were read as esthetically bad. And it's those kinds of misreadings that I see quite a lot as the cultural resistance begins to be known here, and there are other points I could make here.

Also, if you look at some of the books that are coming out here, I think it's inevitable that they will be books specifically oriented towards describing South

Africa for an American audience, that would be received differently in South Africa, that have a function because they connect with American experience. And that's to be expected. Two books that come to mind are Bill Finnegan's *Crossing the Line* [New York: Harper & Row, 1986], about an American teacher, politically relatively naive, who goes over to South Africa and in a situation of crisis describes his education at the hands of the black students. I think that has proved a very popular book in America. Another book is Mark Mathabane's *Kaffir Boy* [New York: Macmillan, 1986], which, after he appeared on the Oprah Winfrey show, has become probably one of the three best-selling books on South Africa ever, and which strikes me as very different from the kind of writing that's coming out from inside the country, in terms of cultural resistance of black writers, but seems to have connected with something in America.

Then one of the points I was going to pick up on was this question of democracy, the chameleon term "democracy," and Njabulo in his piece in *TriQuarterly* talked very eloquently about how it is an unstable notion; and in a certain sense an imported notion of democracy cannot simply be assumed to be automatically popular in South Africa, because the oppressed people have experienced so-called western civilization, western democracy from the position of being deprived of its benefits. So there is quite a considerable degree of resistance to importing a local future in the form of somebody else's present. And even though, from an American perspective, I think South Africa looks historically anachronistic—as people like Njabulo, Hein and Ari have been suggesting—there is this sense that an indigenous notion of democracy, autonomous and authentic in its own way, has to be generated from the grass roots. That's sometimes another of the misalliances that I see in American readings of South Africa and vice versa.

Another example of that: Jesse Jackson and Jerry Falwell, a couple of years ago, were debating on "Nightline." It was one of those moments when I felt that the debate (they were debating the issue of South Africa) was slotted into a very American set of oppositions. At one point Falwell said to Jackson, if the white government falls, won't South Africa degenerate into another Cuba? That's the C-word, O.K.? What was interesting to me was Jesse Jackson's response. He immediately backpedaled and said no, no, no, that won't happen. But there was another response which he could have made, in a different context—it wasn't possible in terms of public debate on mainstream American TV. He could have said, "I have these reservations about human rights in Cuba. But for the majority of South Africans, if they were to wake up in Cuba tomorrow, in terms of achievements in employment, health care, education, housing, they would say 'We're in paradise.'" For me that was a moment where the debate was being refracted through a very American tradition of using a particular rhetoric—and I think that the way Njabulo has talked about democracy, or the way the word "communism" sometimes comes up in the press and is utilized in a very monolithic way, are examples of that.

QUESTIONS AND ANSWERS:

[Some questions were impossible to transcribe in their entirety because of poor recording.]

Question: On the issue of cultural planning, one thing that was obvious is that the majority of the black people in the country might not be aware of the instruments that the oppressive regime is using to further the aims of acculturation to the western mode. For instance, the way Professor Ndebele explained how the miners were reacting, it was very obvious that the miners themselves, due to their circumstances, were not aware of the hidden agenda of those movies, those films, they were shown. Now, since that is the case, it obviously means that the people who are aware of this cultural inadequacy, this cultural ploy by the South African regime, are the intellectuals—people who have actually transcended the illiteracy barrier and are aware of the scheme of the government. Now, in restructuring the culture of the country, it means these people have a heavy load on their shoulders to be the planners of the future culture. I was wondering, since most of our intellectuals, we are educated in the west, and most of the time, even in South Africa, the system of education there has got a lot of western aspects, is it possible that whoever takes upon himself this cultural planning will find that he or she has a bigger problem interpreting correctly what those circumstances require? That is, is the translation into action going to be a reflection of the unaware majority?

Ndebele: I think that what has evolved here, partly, is a question of what an intellectual is. And that is where the problem is. And I think that what we have gained from Ari's intervention is the point that when we talk about the workers, miners, not being aware in the 1920's, we are also mindful that political consciousness has been evolving towards greater and greater awareness over the years. And so we have arrived at a situation where even the working people have a critical attitude towards their own experience. And there's a greater awareness of what the effects of the institutions of oppression, of cultural oppression, on them have been. So, while what we see is that planning for culture does not necessarily depend on the university professor, or other kinds of what you'd call traditional intellectuals, that in fact intellectual activity experiences itself in different forms, in various aspects of the community. And so I think that we need to have a flexible definition of what we mean when we are talking about an intellectual intervention in that context. Certainly, what we see, as Ari was able to show, bears witness to what I'm saying.

M. Kunene: I'm worried about Tim Couzens's conclusion, in that context. It seems to me that his attempt to constitute a formula to describe the worker at that time, is not enough. It is not universal in the context of the workers' attitudes in South Africa. We know too that Ray Phillips, at the time, was really concerned—and others too—with a very small segment of the workers' community. That's the first level of my concern. The second aspect is that there are a lot of people in the mines and in the institutions that are created for them—to escape into work. It does not necessarily mean that they then accept the terms imposed on them by social workers or missionaries or any of those. They may temporarily live under those conditions but they understand that they are not integrated, they are not socialized into that category. That's what I want to say. I don't believe Tim Couzens is terribly accurate.

I have another question here. I am wondering whether we as South African people are not in the danger of being too intellectualist.

The situation in South Africa is very physical at the moment, and requires an emphasis on the physical-political aspects that supersede the cultural and all the theorizing about the culture. I'm just wondering aloud, and I'm hoping that perhaps this could be the last conference that we have of this nature. Perhaps we could put a ban—there are movements that have done this—on conferences, a ban on discussing intellectually in the abstract. And then perhaps we could meet after three years to evaluate the results of our experiment, in terms of intellectual guidelines that we want people to follow. I think there is perhaps an excessive praise for our activities as "intellectuals," which I think is very dangerous for us. We get too much praise...for books and analysis. South Africa seems really to have produced just merely surface materials. It's not enough. I think perhaps the talking tends to masturbate us. I'm just thinking aloud.

Ndebele: Well, obviously I don't share Professor Kunene's view. I also detected earlier this morning an anti-intellectual attitude, which I don't share. I think that the nature of the struggle in South Africa also involves the level of ideas. And conferences, in my view—the fact that they take place far away from home might be a problem. But they also take place inside the country as well, and reflection has to take place on the action that people engage in, and no one can claim that there is no role to the intellectual struggle. Certainly we have universities also in the country where students are trying to grapple with the ideas that are being thrown at them. And lecturers and other intellectuals in that context are trying to demystify and get rid of impressions which people over the years internalize and which condition their behavior. So I'm suspicious, sometimes, of the anti-intellectualism that sometimes rears its head, because I'm not sure that not being an intellectual and saying something against it necessarily makes you a revolutionary. I think that what I am

111

aware of that is taking place at home is a humility to listen to each other. Ari was talking earlier, and also Alfred, that there is consultation, ideas are discussed, there is a healthy debate that is taking place in which people accept that what they have to say is not inherently more valuable than another person's view. The question is to listen to what somebody else is saying and respond to him at that level. There are people in here who are willing to bare their souls and risk their sincerity, expecting that there will be a similar response to their insights. And an anti-intellectual stance might serve to mystify and continue the misunderstanding, and the clouding of issues, that we see in South Africa today. When Hein makes reference to the use of new words, it's part and parcel of that context. And it emerges out of the history of reflection. So we should not be told that intellectual activities have no role to play. I think they have a lot of roles to play, and even more so now, when sometimes it might be said that they don't have a role to play. When we get to a stage where people feel that there's too much intellectualization, really that is precisely when there is a need for even more reflection. So I don't agree with Professor Kunene on that view. But of course he is entitled to his view.

The other issue that I want to make reference to is that I did point out that my reference to Peter Horn and to Couzens is not necessarily uncritical. I would be the first to agree with Professor Mazisi Kunene that indeed not all the workers in the mines were bought by this. But what I was trying to suggest was that sometimes activities of this nature do cause ambiguity, do cause some confusion, which over a period of time has to be subjected to reflection, and that people have to be given the opportunity to clarify their ideas. I'm not suggesting at all that everybody bought these films, or was bought by them. On the contrary, there were many people who were able to see through activities of this nature.

M. Kunene: I think there was a gross misunderstanding here of what I said. I'm not at all anti-intellectual. I think intellectuals have got a role, much more so now in South Africa, where there has been an emphasis purely on the victim as an emotional being, without a brain, but who is hammered from all sides by the government. I think there is a renaissance of the cultural kind, of an intellectual kind, in South Africa. But having said that, I think I'm talking about my feeling about myself: I'm not too happy at my cleverness. And what I said was not directed at Professor Ndebele's statement, a statement I respect very deeply—there should be no mistake about that. But I'm saying that there is a physical situation in South Africa, and sometimes when we are exposed to conferences such as this one, in which there is a discussion only of the cultural aspect—the spiritual aspect—we tend to make a greater emphasis on that, much more than the physical aspect. Maybe it would have been useful for us to have had a political speech, so that we have all these discussions in context, in a relationship which Professor Ndebele himself referred to as a full, existential relationship between politics and culture. These things have to be seen in this context. And I am amazed to think that I could really be labeled or characterized as anti-intellectual. I am all for intellectuals! I like them very much! [Laughter.]

Willemse: I would like to think about something Mazisi has said. He has come up with a certain definition, namely that he demarcates culture and politics. I would argue that the cultural action is very much in the forefront of action. Even when one is talking about physical action, in terms of politics, it indicates cultural action as well. I don't think that one can readily make that distinction between culture on the one hand and politics on the other. I would be in deep trouble if I tried to separate them.

M. Kunene: I didn't! [Laughter.]

Question: How do you start planning for the future of South Africa politically and culturally when at present you still have problems in South Africa?

Ndebele: When you are talking about planning for the future, if you are engaged in an attempt to understand the present, the logical process is to speculate what the implications of that understanding are likely to be. But it does not necessarily follow that what you say is going to happen, is going to happen that way. All that one is trying to suggest is that in thinking about the future you can make meaning of the present. In other words, thinking about the future is also an attempt to get a sense of what is happening right now. And what you say is likely to happen may not necessarily happen exactly that way; so projecting yourself into the future, it seems to me, is a tactical way—and I regard it as such—of attempting to understand more the dynamics of the present. So this is particularly evident when people come up with programs of action. Programs of action are an attempt to deal with solutions, to come up with solutions of the moment, which have implications for the future. So if we are talking about a future of democracy, we have to say something to concretize our image of what democracy actually means; and I think when people talk about the future, it should be in this context.

Gibbons: I'm not sure I have a right to respond to that question, but I'd like to. One of the principal attractions of the *TriQuarterly* volume, to me, was that the sense of the future seemed buried in it. It did not seem inaccessible in many ways; it seemed as if models of discourse between languages, cultures, races, models of democratic expression, models of democratic social organization, were present, either explicitly in some sorts of works in the volume, or implicitly carried in the textures of other kinds of fiction and poetry which were striving to create, as many people have said, images of

114

an alternative future. It seems to me as a reader that images of an alternative future often seem to be discernible in the images already available in the present. It's just a matter of finding them, recognizing them, and then—if I can presume to speak completely from the outside—of trying to do whatever you can to nurture them so that they become the ones which grow, and are not pushed aside or stamped out or replaced by something which is worse, something which also already exists and also has a claim on the future which we would want to deny. So it doesn't seem to me to be a question—as others have said—of imagining something that would come out of nowhere. It's a question of looking at what has already been produced. In this case the concrete examples are poems and stories and some essays and photographs and artworks, and one tries to synthesize them in one's own mind as a reader searching for that future which I am convinced lies there.

D. P. Kunene: First, there are many predictable things that may be future—and I put it in quotes, "predictable." Secondly, the future is not something that is not here now—it is here with us and in fact some things that are being done now are done precisely because that future, wherever it may be, is predictable. It's predictable—things are being done, for example, to try to take care of some of the problems that occur because children are missing education. Because there is so much time that is lost in education. Because there is so much disruption, and these people are growing, their time is getting wasted—what is going to happen to them? One can predict what is going to happen to children who are being tortured in detention. I don't know how many people have seen here the film *Witness to Apartheid.* The horror of these things—you can predict what the emotional destabilization and the social destabilization resulting from the lack of education is going to be. I think it is very, very important that we throw our minds now and again into that time when some of these problems will

115

be with us, but also—to come back to the question—the future, by the way, is not something that's going to be after twelve midnight on such and such a date. It is together with the present.

Bunn: I'd like to support that strongly, and support what's been said about planning for the future. Because I really think the question of culture is also a political question, and planning for the future is a political act. Unless one does that, one is locked into a reactive position—which is precisely the sort of thing that the South African government wants. This extends to the question of literature as well. There is a certain type of South African literature which is locked into the problem or the image of apocalypse. And when I think of planning for the future, I think of planning in terms of something constructive, something utopian even, in a positive sense; the image of apocalypse doesn't really enter my mind.

Question: What I'm surprised about is what some speakers mentioned about women writing. I was wondering why you didn't have African women writers represented at this conference. Is it a problem that you can't find women writers?

Gibbons: I suppose I should answer that. I think there are two parts to my answer. First, in the planning of the issue, it was very much on our minds, and after the issue had gone to press, I'm sorry to say, I found a contact that we'd never found during the time of preparation. And there was a difficulty in getting manuscripts—perhaps one of the other editors could address that also—from black African women writers. There's a second part to the answer: there was a woman scheduled to be here with us who was not able to come, at the very last minute, and that was a great disappointment, but was something over which we had no control, and over which she had no control either. Perhaps more than that I shouldn't say. But that's a very real concern that's been in many minds here, although we were not able to remedy it. I don't think my answer is satisfactory; it's just that it's the only answer I have.

Bunn: We have two women South African writers here.

Gibbons [to audience]: But you mean a *black* woman writer.

Question: Yes.

Bunn: But I think we've been addressing this question in a number of the sessions. Nise Malange was one of the writers who was going to be here. But yes, I think we should address it more.

Question: I'd like to make a comment about how much of what's happening in South Africa and South African literature is read in the United States. I think the comment about Jesse Jackson is very real and important in terms of understanding what happens in this country. I'd like to also pick up on what you were saying [to Mazisi Kunene] about its happening on a very physical level in South Africa. Obviously in the United States there is a constant cry, with the hegemony of Reaganism, for "Isn't there another way? Can't we settle this reasonably around the table?" But it's happening on a very physical level. It's not a question of what anybody wants, it's what's actually happening. In this country, while on the one hand there's a very moralistic outpouring of sentiment around the divestiture movement, around the stock business, when it comes to an armed struggle for national liberation, or a confrontation to overturn the violence that's experienced every day, the United States is being propped up to take the moralistic position against that. And not only against that process of liberation, but also a moralistic position against what is likely to be the early period of any new regime. After

117

all, the word "utopia" does mean "nowhere." And we're not talking about that, we're talking about the real world. And consequently, it seems to me, in the United States there's a very difficult time ahead of us. In Vietnam it happened, it happens in Central America—that people are propped up by the ruling elite in this country to take a position against what is objectively happening in the world, in favor of some utopian, moralistic view which has no relationship to what's actually going on. So it seems to me that we have to be very careful about ignoring the fact, in any meeting like this, that there in fact is an armed struggle going on right now, that people are engaged in war. And it's that war that serves as the context for everything that every intellectual says. Obviously, to be at Northwestern University, and to make a comment about intellectuals, is not to be popular, right? In other words, this is a kind of self-serving response that many academics have. But the fact is that, in the world, the discussion of South Africa is being determined by the nature of the popular war of resistance that is going on. And it seems to me that we in the United States have to prepare ourselves to resist the moralism of the right wing, that will stand up to take a position against any regime that is likely to emerge. And it seems to me that in these conferences we have to constantly remind ourselves that it is the people of South Africa who will determine the future of South Africa, and our response in this country is to stop the U.S. government and to stop Reaganism, and the Democratic party, from assisting any forces of evil in South Africa and anywhere in the world.

Nixon: I'd like to add something to that. It goes without saying that when I was talking earlier about how South African issues are inevitably refracted through American concerns, that the history in this country of the civil rights struggle, and the continuing struggle against racism in this country, has helped the South African issue gain emotional momentum and organized momentum, with very considerable progress. But some other issues around South Africa are much more difficult to attach to American concerns. And one of those, for instance—I mention it because it's coming up in the next year—is the issue of Mozambique. We've recently seen aid go from the Reagan administration to the UNITA [National Union for the Total Independence of Angola] movement. One of the big actions around South Africa in Congress in the next year is going to be a very intense right-wing lobby to try to recognize the MNR [Mozambique National Resistance—also known as RENAMO] as a kind of contra movement in Mozambique. And, talking to people prominent in the antiapartheid movement here, one of the real challenges they're facing at the moment is to get Americans aware of the regional conflict—in other words, South African imperialism, regional imperialism. And particularly what's going on in Mozambique at the moment. And the real tragedy, if millions of dollars go to the MNR, and it accrues a kind of contra-like aura, is that you will see effects as devastating as those in Nicaragua.

McClintock: I wanted to respond to the earlier question about the absence of women's writing. There is an extraordinary disproportion between the prominence of black women and white women in South Africa in the struggles against apartheid. The most successful antipass demonstration was the Women's March on Pretoria in the fifties. Women have been at the forefront of almost every single political struggle, in rent and bus boycotts, in the politics of education, in civic resistance, and so on. It seems at the moment that there is a very urgent sense of the need to bring women into the trade-union movements, into federations, into cultural organizations, into positions of prominence in education. The National Federation of South African Women is as eminent as seems possible. But on the other hand, despite this extraordinary political participation of women, there is this dearth of representation of women at the cultural level. And I think that the reasons for this are profoundly social and profoundly historical, and are not going to be able to be wished away by the best gestures and the best intentions of a conference such as this. And our obligations are to go back and reach into what those historical conditions are, and then work forward. I think I mentioned a few of them this morning. I think they're intricate and many. Some of them are the kind of obstacles that have faced women internationally, that have kept them hidden from history, in voicing their own experience, their own narratives, in any published form. The others are the conditions of women's lives that make it extraordinarily difficult to participate in communal cultural activity, if they are burdened with child care, domestic work and so on.

But the point that I wanted to make was that women have faced the problem of the absence of this kind of cultural representation, they faced the lack of prominent women figures from which to learn and from which to gain legitimacy and the confidence to speak. But on the other hand there's a kind of a curious paradoxical strength that I think is emerging from that. And Jane Taylor today mentioned Ellen Kuzwayo's autobiography and a recently emerged autobiographical sense in women's writing.

One other novel I would like to mention is a collaborative cultural venture between a black woman and an Afrikaans woman, which emerged in this book called *Poppie Nongena* [London: Hodder and Stoughton, 1980]. Now that, I think, demonstrates very forcibly the kinds of complexities of the situation: the black woman chose to remain anonymous, she told her story—which was the story of her family's plight, and her own plight, during the rebellion, and she told it to Elsa Joubert, a fairly well-known Afrikaans writer. But she chose to remain anonymous. The way the novel has been packaged, even though it is an absolutely collaborative venture, and is a story based on the oral history of a black woman, is called "*Poppie Nongena* by Elsa Joubert." The voice and the participation of the black woman have been relatively obscured—I think in a very crippling fashion. But on the other hand this novel in itself, in the attempt of being a collaboration, is of a different kind than any other cultural form that you've had in South Africa. Ellen Kuzwayo's autobiography shares the same feature. Jane mentioned the kind of criticisms that the autobiography faced, which other male black autobiographies did not face: "Why is she dwelling on her own personal experience?" And yet, if you look at the autobiography, it is quite different from other, male, autobiographies, such as Abrahams's [Peter Abrahams, *Tell Freedom*, New York: Knopf, 1954]. The male autobiographies typically begin with "I." Kuzwayo's first three chapters have to do with women in general. And it is only in the fourth chapter that she begins to talk about her own personal background and her own experiences. So my point is that despite the absence of figures for women to turn to—individual figures—women facing that dilemma are perhaps doing something different, and are producing very collaborative work and reaching out into a communal sense of "we" as opposed to an individual "I," an individual story that is going to be elaborated. And I think even though we're standing in a position of extraordinary imbalance, perhaps even out of that position we're going to have quite soon a very resurgent sense of a different kind of aspiration.

Question: There are black researchers researching South African female fiction. And it might prove useful, at some time, for people to have access to the voice of the other's other, rather than hearing articulated an interpretation of that particular fiction by people whose proclivities and dispositions towards that literature are quite strikingly different from my own. But the problem is that black females essentially, in this country, fail to have access to the modes of production and the support that some other people do. And as long as that continues to be the case, then there will be many silent voices.

NOTES ON PARTICIPANTS

David Bunn is co-editor of *From South Africa* (*TriQuarterly* #69). A lecturer in the English Department at the University of the Western Cape, he obtained a Ph.D. in English literature from Northwestern University in 1987, writing a dissertation entitled "Embodying Africa: Description, Ideology, Imperialism and the Colonial Romance."

Neville Choonoo is a professor of Afro-American and African literature at SUNY-Oneonta, in New York State. He has developed comparative studies of black American and South African literature and published articles on black South African autobiography. He formerly taught at the University of Durban, Westville.

Ingrid de Kok lives in Cape Town and works for Khanya College, an independent, progressive educational instutution, a project of SACHED, the South African Committee for Higher Education. Her poetry has appeared in journals in Canada and South Africa and in *LIP*, an anthology of South African women's writing. Her first book of poems, *Familiar Ground*, was published in 1988 (Johannesburg, Ravan).

Keorapetse Kgositsile has taught at the universities of Dar Es Salaam, Nairobi and Gabarone. A journalist by profession, he worked with the Columbia University Writing Program in the mid-seventies, and later with *Black Dialogue Magazine* in New York. His volumes of poetry include *My Name is Afrika* (Garden City, NY: Doubleday, 1971), *The Present is a Dangerous Place to Live* (Chicago: Third World Press, 1974) and *Herzpuren* (Schwifting, West Germany: Schwiftinger Galerie-Verlag, 1980). He is a cultural officer of the African National Congress, living in exile in Zambia.

Daniel P. Kunene is a professor of African languages and literature at the University of Wisconsin, Madison. His books include *Heroic Poetry of the Basotho* (Oxford, England: Clarendon, 1971); two volumes of poetry, *Pirates Have Become Our Kings* (East African Publishing House, 1979) and *A Seed Must Seem to Die* (Johannesburg: Ravan, 1981); and a collection of short stories, *From the Pit of Hell to the Spring of Life* (Johannesburg: Ravan, 1986). Kunene has translated several books into English, including *The Works of Thomas Mofolo* (Los Angeles: African Studies Center, University of California, Los Angeles, 1967). He has also taught at the University of Cape Town and at UCLA.

Mazisi Kunene was a founding member of the Anti-Apartheid Movement in Great Britain and has represented the African National Congress in Europe and the U.S. The authoritative Zulu poet, he has published two epic poems, *Emperor Shaka the Great* (London: Heinemann, 1979) and *Anthem of the Decades* (London: Heinemann, 1981), and two volumes of poetry, *Zulu Poems* (London: André Deutsch, 1970) and *The Ancestors and the Sacred Mountain* (London: Heinemann, African writers series, 1982).

Anne McClintock is a candidate for a Ph.D. in English literature at Columbia University. She is the author of a monograph on Simone de Beauvoir and is working on a dissertation on race and gender in British imperial culture. She has published articles in *Critical Inquiry* and other journals.

Njabulo S. Ndebele won the Noma Award in 1984 for his book, *Fools and Other Stories* (Johannesburg: Ravan, 1983), a collection of short stories set in Charterston Location, the township where he grew up. In both his criticism and fiction, he is concerned with the cultural oppression which succeeds colonialism. He has been a lecturer in African, Afro-American and English literature at the University College of Roma, Lesotho. Since the conference, he has assumed the position of Pro-Vice Chancellor of the National University of Lesotho.

Rob Nixon is a candidate for a Ph.D. in English literature at Columbia University. He is conducting research in topics of exile and third-world metropolitan relations in the writing of V. S. and Shiva Naipaul. He has published articles on South African literature and culture in *Critical Inquiry,* the *Village Voice,* and *Grand Street.*

Alfred Temba Qabula is a union organizer and oral poet, whose performances at workers' gatherings in Natal have led to a revival of the *imbongi,* or praise-singer, tradition of Nguni poetry. In 1983 Qabula helped develop the "Dunlop Play," a play about worker history created by rubber factory workers. He is a founder of the Durban Workers' Cultural Local and of the Trade Union and Cultural Centre in Clairwood.

Sheila Roberts's first collection of short stories, *Outside Life's Feast* (Johannesburg: Ad. Donker, 1975), won the Olive Schreiner Prize. Her other books include a volume of poetry, *Dialogues and Divertimenti* (Johannesburg: Ad. Donker,1985); two novels, *The Weekenders* (Johannesburg: Bateleur Press, 1981) and *He's My Brother* (Johannesburg: Ad. Donker, 1977), published in the U. S. as *Johannesburg Requiem* (New York: Taplinger, 1980); and her most recent collection of stories, *This Time of Year* (Johannesburg: Ad. Donker, 1983). She is a professor of English at the University of Wisconsin, Milwaukee.

Ari Sitas is a founder of the Junction Avenue Theatre Company in Johannesburg and an organizer of the workers' theater movement. Sitas has worked closely with COSATU, the confederation of trade unions. He lectures in industrial sociology at the University of Natal and is an editor of the *South African Labour Bulletin*. He edited *Black Mamba Rising*, an anthology of workers' poetry (Natal: University of Natal/COSATU Worker's Cultural Local, 1986).

Jane Taylor, co-editor of *From South Africa*, lectures in the English Department at the University of the Western Cape. She was formerly employed as an editor with McDougal Littell, an Illinois publishing firm. The Introduction that she and David Bunn wrote for *From South Africa* has been selected to appear in an anthology of theoretical writing to be published in South Africa.

Hein Willemse is a senior lecturer at the University of the Western Cape. He is a member of Vakalisa, a progressive Western Cape artists' collective that compiles and publishes new artistic materials, from poetry to graphics. His collections of poetry are *Angsland* (South Africa: BLAC Publishing House, 1981) and *Die Lê van die Land* (1987). He is co-editor of *Swart Africaans Skrywers* (1986) and *Die Trojaanse Perd* (Emmarentia, South Africa: Taurus, 1986).

Nise Malange, the Durban worker poet, who was to have participated in this conference, could not complete travel arrangements.

FROM SOUTH AFRICA POSTER

The above "Noah's Ark" linocut by John Muafangejo, which appeared in *TriQuarterly* #69 (*From South Africa*), has been reproduced as a 24″ X 36″ black-and-red poster, printed on ivory, textured stock, in a limited edition of 300 copies. The poster is available from *TriQuarterly* for $11.00, which includes postage and handling. Send your orders, with payment, to *TriQuarterly*, 2020 Ridge Ave., Evanston, IL 60208.

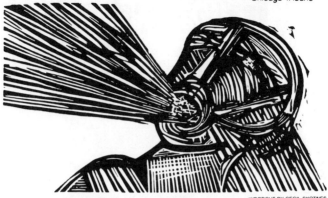

TriQuarterly

Fiction • Poetry • Art • Criticism
Three times a year

*Illustration by
Matthew Owens
TQ #58*

The New York Times has called **TriQuarterly** "perhaps the pre-eminent journal for literary fiction" in the nation. **Chicago** magazine describes it as "one of the best, issue after issue." But see for yourself—subscribe now . . .